WIZARD'S
SUPERMARKET SCIENCE

illustrated by Roy McKie

Contents

Mr.

by Don Herbert

Random House 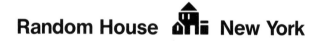 **New York**

Text Copyright © 1980 by Don Herbert. Illustrations Copyright © 1980 by Roy McKie.
All rights reserved under International and Pan-American Copyright Conventions.
Published in the United States by Random House, Inc., New York, and simultaneously
in Canada by Random House of Canada Limited, Toronto.

Library of Congress Cataloging in Publication Data:
Herbert, Don. Mr. Wizard's supermarket science. Includes index.
SUMMARY: Gives directions for about 100 simple experiments using items
available in the supermarket. Includes explanations of the scientific
principles demonstrated.   1. Science—Experiments—Juvenile literature.
[1. Science—Experiments.   2. Experiments]   I. McKie, Roy.
II. Title. Q164.H48   507'.8   79-27217   ISBN: 0-394-83800-9 (pbk.);
0-394-93800-3 (lib. bdg.)   Manufactured in the United States of America

25 26 27 28 29 30

Salad Dressing

Cleaning Supplies

Dairy

Meats

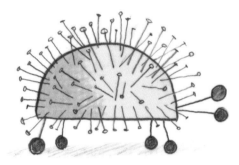

Introduction

Hidden on the shelves of your supermarket are hundreds of tricks, stunts, games, puzzles, and pieces of scientific apparatus. After you read this book, you'll walk down the aisle, see a bottle of vinegar, and think "fuel" for a rocket! Dried peas? Joints for a construction set! A rolling pin? The key to encode and decode secret messages!

Collecting ideas for using household objects to do odd and entertaining things was part of my preparation for the *Mr. Wizard* television show. Each week for more than fifteen years on NBC, a boy or girl came over to my "house" to have fun playing around with science. As a result, I've collected file drawers full of suggestions for having fun with everyday equipment. Those you can do with supermarket items are the basis for this book.

One of the reasons many people will be surprised when you do some of the activities in this book (make a straw into an oboe, for instance), is that they think of objects with "functional fixedness."

This term was originated by Dr. Karl Dunker after he challenged some of his students to attach a candle at eye level to a door. They could use only these items on a nearby table:

Only a few of the students were able to solve the problem.

Then he challenged a new group of students. The same equipment was on the table, but with this difference:

Many more students were able to figure out the answer.

You see, the first group saw each box only as a *container*. The primary use for the box became fixed in their minds. The students' *functional fixedness* prevented them from thinking of the box in any other way.

The second group saw the empty boxes and found it much easier to recognize and use the normally unimportant properties of a box to solve the problem. You'll find out how they did it on page 91.

As you mentally go down the aisles of these pages, you'll begin to think of items on the shelves of your supermarket with "functional freedom," because in almost all of the suggestions you use common things in uncommon ways—that's one of the reasons the stunts are interesting and fun to do.

Now and then you'll need to cut, heat, ignite, or punch a hole in something. Scissors, knives, matches, and stoves are useful tools but should always be handled carefully. If you haven't used the tools or the stove before or aren't sure how to use them, ask an adult to help you do it safely.

If a trick doesn't work the first time, try to figure out why by re-reading it and noting the scientific principle involved. Sometimes only a slight change in the way you do it will make all the difference.

So take out your imaginary shopping cart and get ready to fill it with ideas for having fun with supermarket science!

Breakfast Foods

Cereal-Box Camera Obscura

You can't see through a cereal box, and that means that an empty, closed-up box is dark inside. You can make it into a camera obscura, an ancient device for viewing the world in miniature—and in living color!

Remove the waxed-paper lining from a family-size cereal box that is at least 12 inches tall. If you can't find one that big, substitute a large soap-powder box.

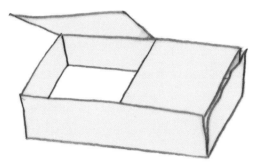

With scissors or a sharp knife, cut across the middle of the front of the box, along the side edge to the bottom, and then across the bottom to produce a flap.

Fold the flap back. Cut a piece of waxed paper the same size as the bottom of the box. Tape it inside the box across the width about 2 inches above the bottom. Use waxed paper from a roll, not from the cereal-box liner. The liner is not transparent enough and probably too creased.

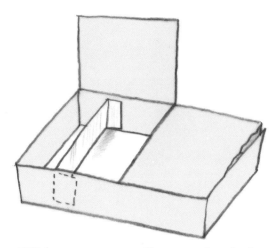

With a pin or needle, punch a hole in the middle of the bottom of the box. Close the flap and tape it back into its original position with masking tape. Be sure no light can leak in around the tape.

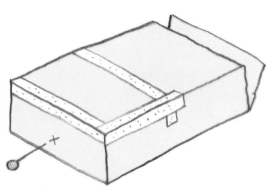

With the scissors, cut off the flaps from the top of the box and then cut indentations into the sides to more or less conform to the shape of your forehead and nose.

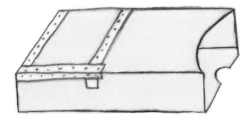

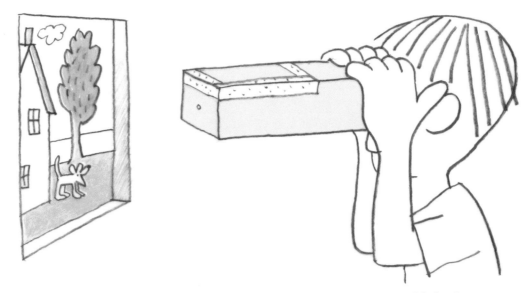

Stand in front of a window outside of which is a sunlit scene. Hold the box up to your eyes and point the pinhole through the window at the scene. Cup your hands around the sides of the box and your eyes to keep out as much light as possible.

You'll see the scene outside the window in miniature inside the box!

The pinhole acts as a simple lens which projects the view outside the window onto the waxed-paper screen near the bottom of the box. The image is small, fairly dim, upside down, but in color.

If you enlarge the hole, you'll make the image brighter, but also less sharp.

Your eyes can focus on something no closer than about 10 inches—that's why the scene has to be at least that far away, and why the box has to be so tall.

The camera obscura was known back in Greek times. In a completely darkened room, a small hole in one wall projected the image of the scene outside onto the opposite wall. Artists often traced the image of a scene prior to painting it. Astronomers have used the technique to project images of the sun, moon, and brighter stars. Camera obscura means dark room in Latin.

Photographers have developed the idea into a real camera by arranging for the projected image to expose film. Books in the library have detailed instructions on how to photograph with a pinhole camera.

Cereal-Box Planetarium

Do you like to go to bed under the stars? It's easy to do with an empty cereal box, a pencil, and a flashlight!

With the pencil, punch holes in one end of the cereal box in the pattern of the stars in the sky. Shine a strong flashlight through the holes onto the ceiling of your bedroom.

A good start would be the Big and Little Dippers (Ursa Major and Ursa Minor) because they look like actual dippers.

An encyclopedia or book on stars will show you how to lay out the stars in other important constellations.

You'll probably remember the constellations and the stars in them more easily once you've prepared your cereal-box planetarium.

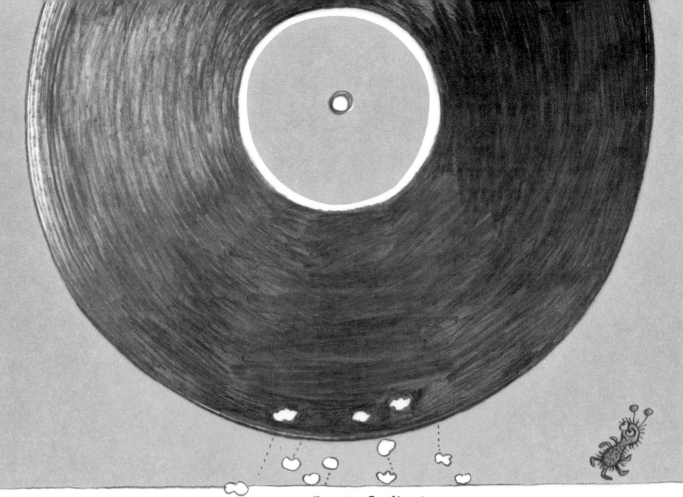

Cereal Static Indicator

The weight of your puffed cereal doesn't matter much when you eat it, but the fact that it weighs so little makes it a good indicator of static electricity.

Rub a phonograph record with wool, perhaps a scarf or a sweater. Then hold the edge of the record above fine, dry, light puffed cereal. Some of the cereal jumps up to the record and then hops off!

As you rub the record with the wool, you transfer tiny bits of negative electricity called electrons from the wool onto the record. Ordinarily, electrons repel each other, and they spread out as far from each other as possible. But because the record is a nonconductor of electricity, the electrons stay where you put them. They are "static" electricity.

The extra electrons on the record attract pieces of the cereal which ordinarily have no electrical charge. When the cereal touches the record, electrons on the record are transferred to some of the pieces of cereal. Because both the cereal and the record now have the same negative charge, they repel each other. You can't notice any movement of the record, but you certainly can see the cereal jump up and down.

As you take the record in and out of its paper cover, you may also transfer electrons from the paper onto the record surface. The static charge attracts dirt and dust which produce a popping sound when you play the record. With a special cloth or brush and an anti-static liquid, you can remove the dirt as well as the static electricity.

Dried Foods

Spaghetti: Mothball Substitute

You can use spaghetti as a substitute for mothballs—not for keeping moths away, but as an important part of an unusual centerpiece for a party!

Years ago mothballs were made of naphthalene. When you put them in a tall glass of water and added secret ingredients, the mothballs kept rising to the top and then sinking to the bottom for as long as half an hour! This made a terrific-looking centerpiece.

Then manufacturers began making mothballs out of paradichlorobenzene. The new mothballs were slightly lighter in weight than the old ones. Once they rose to the surface of the water, they stayed there!

After trying raisins, beans, peas, nuts, grapes, and scores of other items, the best substitute for the old mothballs turned out to be spaghetti!

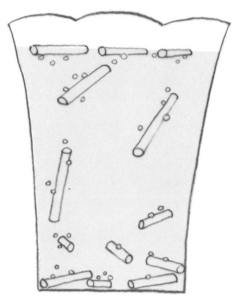

Into a tall glass containing 2 cups of water stir 1 tablespoon of baking soda until it dissolves. Break uncooked spaghetti into 1-inch pieces and put them into the glass. They will sink to the bottom of the glass. Then stir in 3 tablespoons of vinegar.

A chemical reaction produces carbon dioxide gas which forms bubbles on the pieces of spaghetti at the bottom of the glass. The bubbles float the pieces to the top. There the bubbles break, sending the pieces back to the bottom. When the action starts to slow down, add a few more tablespoons of vinegar.

Setting up the display in a large glass dish or vase (increasing the amount of ingredients in the same proportion) makes it into a conversation piece for a party. Add food coloring to the water to make it match the rest of the decorations.

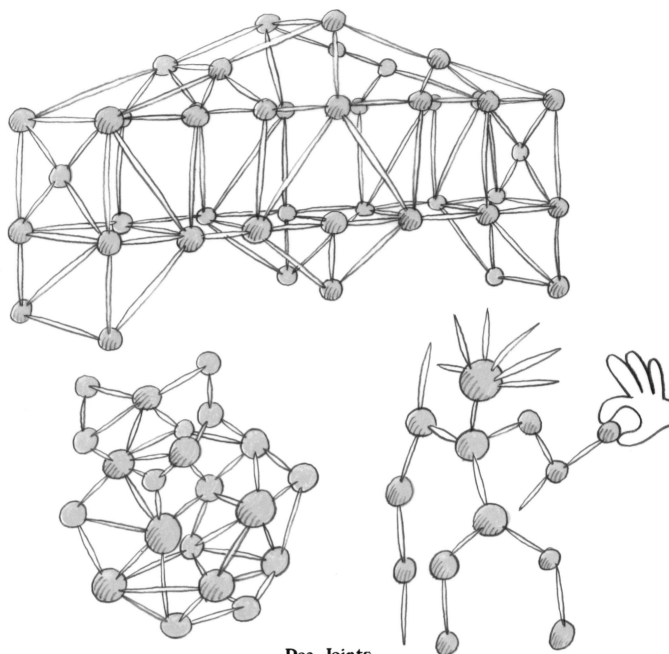

Pea Joints

When peas dry, they shrink. Soak them in water and they'll swell. This property makes them ideal for the joints of a child's construction set, all the parts of which are in the supermarket: dried peas and toothpicks!

Soak dried peas overnight. Using toothpicks as the structural members and the softened peas as the joints, you can build almost anything—bridges, buildings, toys, figures, molecules, abstract shapes, geometric designs, and so on.

When you're through, allow a day or two for the peas to dry out again. They'll shrink and hold the toothpicks firmly in place!

Bag of Beans

A popular homemade toy is a bean bag. Partly fill a small cloth bag with dried beans or peas and sew it shut. You can toss it around the room because the confined mass of small, hard seeds can shift within the bag and absorb the impact of landing.

Make several of different sizes and toss them at targets such as holes cut in a cardboard box.

Photographers have found bean bags useful for supporting long lenses. A larger version of a bean bag is placed on a support and the lens is nestled into a dent made in the top surface of the bag. You can steady binoculars or a telescope in the same way.

How Many Peas?

You've probably taken part in that popular guessing contest in which you estimate how many small things are in a jar. Whoever comes closest to the actual total wins a prize. You can play the game at home (at a birthday party, for instance) with a bag of dried peas or beans.

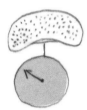

How do you find out how many are actually in the package? You can count each one, of course; but as the saying goes, there must be an easier way! There is. Weigh them.

Weigh the package of peas on any scale that indicates ounces or grams. Then weigh a small cup. Fill it with peas and weigh it again. Subtract the weight of the cup to find the weight of the peas. Count the peas in the cup. Divide the total weight of the package of peas by the weight of the sample. Multiply your answer by the number of peas in the sample to find the total number of peas in the package.

Soups

Moldy Soup

You eat tomato soup because you like the flavor and it's good for you. The next time you open a can, save some of the soup to start a garden in which to plant invisible "seeds"!

How can you plant the "seeds" if they're invisible? Just follow the instructions, and in a few days you'll have so many millions of plants, you will be able to see them easily enough. Look at them with a magnifying glass and you'll marvel at the beautiful and unusual plants called molds.

Open a can of tomato soup and pour a few table-spoons into each of several small dishes. Sprinkle bread crumbs onto the soup in one dish. Scrape your finger over the floor and then dip it into the soup in another dish. Sprinkle a pinch of soil into a third.

What you're doing is collecting invisible mold "seeds" called spores (which are almost everywhere) and transferring them to the soup.

Cover the dishes with plastic wrap and put them in a warm, dark place for several days.

Soon you'll see spots of mold on the surface of the soup. Each spot will probably have been started by a single mold spore. When the conditions were right for its growth, it used the soup for food and produced more spores. They fell on nearby parts of the soup and grew into new plants. In a few days there were enough plants for you to see.

Look at the molds closely with a magnifying glass. You'll see various colors and shapes. If you look them up in a book of molds, you'll probably be able to identify such common ones as *Mucor*, *Rhizopus*, *Aspergillus*, and *Penicillium* (from which the antibiotic penicillin was first extracted).

You can grow molds more scientifically (perhaps for a science project) by sterilizing all the equipment and keeping records of where and to what you exposed the soup.

Baking Ingredients

Soda Fountain

Baking soda (chemical name: sodium bicarbonate) is an important ingredient in the preparation of cookies, biscuits, and cakes. It's also an important ingredient for making a soda "fountain"!

In 2 cups of water in a tall bottle, dissolve 1 tablespoon of baking soda and a few drops of liquid detergent or a pinch of soap powder. Then pour in a few tablespoons of vinegar. The chemical reaction produces tiny soap bubbles filled with carbon dioxide gas. The foam rises up and flows over the top of the bottle in a fountain of bubbles.

Baking soda dissolved in water reacts with acids like vinegar and sour milk to produce carbon dioxide gas. In cooking, the gas bubbles in the dough make the final baked goods lighter in texture.

Baking soda is also one of the main ingredients in baking powders which act in a similar way.

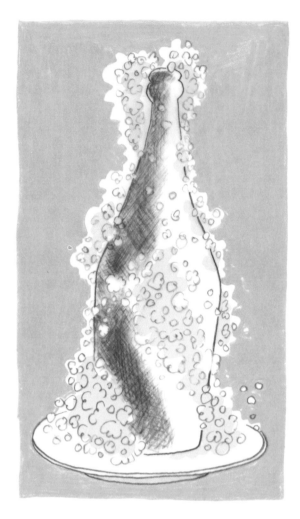

Baking (?) Soda

Baking soda is one of the few chemically pure substances in the supermarket and is amazingly versatile.

Because it's a base (the opposite of an acid) in water, you can dissolve a tea-

spoon of it in water and drink it to counteract the effects of excess stomach acidity.

It's made up of very fine particles, which in paste form act as a mild abrasive for cleaning teeth as well as countertops and pans. If you get rosin on your hands from an evergreen tree (at Christmas for instance), wet your hands, rub the spot of rosin with baking soda, and then rinse. The rosin will be gone.

In dry form, baking soda absorbs moisture as well as chemical vapors that may be in the air. That's why it works as a deodorizer in the refrigerator.

Soda Fire-Fighter

Baking soda doesn't burn. Heating it releases carbon dioxide which doesn't burn either. That's why baking soda is sprinkled on grease and oil fires to put them out.

It's also one of the main ingredients in the so-called soda-acid fire extinguishers. You can make your own version out of a large jar with a metal screw top and an olive bottle.

Dissolve 2 tablespoons of baking soda in 2 cups of water and pour into the large jar. Fill the olive bottle with vinegar and place it in the jar. The top of the olive bottle must be above the level of the water.

With an ice pick or a hammer and nail, punch a large hole in the cover of the big jar. Screw the cover back on the jar. Now turn the jar upside down and gently shake it. The chemical reaction produces carbon dioxide gas which forces the solution out of the hole.

The same reaction is what forces the water out of the professional soda-acid extinguisher. Inside is water with sodium bicarbonate dissolved in it and a container of acid. When you turn the extinguisher upside down, the pressure forces the water out of the nozzle. The fire is put out because the water cools off the fuel and the carbon dioxide gas dissolved in the water is released, smothering the flames.

Paste-ry

Bread is "glued" together by a material called gluten which is formed from the proteins in flour. Since ancient times, the stickiness of gluten has been used to paste things together.

If you're in a hurry, make a paste that will hold pieces of paper together reasonably well by simply adding flour a little at a time to water. Then stir with a fork or spoon until it is free of lumps and about the consistency of thick pancake batter.

Make a better paste by first heating the water to which you will add the flour. Be sure you are familiar with the way your stove works before you do this. If you are not, ask an adult to help you.

When the water is very hot, slowly add 1 cup of very hot water to ½ cup of flour, stirring until the mixture is smooth. Simmer for a few minutes. The hot water dissolves more of the gluten, which improves the holding power. When the paste is cool, it is ready to use. Store it in a screw-top jar to prevent it from drying out and becoming hard as a rock.

Rye-Bread Wallpaper Cleaner

The stickiness of gluten is the reason it is used in wallpaper cleaner. Rye flour contains gluten. You can lift light soil from wallpaper by rubbing it with a slice of rye bread.

Dough "Clay"

The fact that gluten dries to a hard material makes it a good substitute for modeling clay.

Mix 1½ cups of flour with ½ cup of salt. Then slowly add ½ cup of water and ¼ cup of vegetable oil, kneading the dough until the ingredients are thoroughly mixed. If the dough's too sticky, add more flour. Use the dough clay in the same manner as real clay. When you're finished, set the finished work aside for a few days to harden. If you're in a hurry, bake it for several hours in an oven set at 250 degrees Fahrenheit (121 degrees Celsius). Before you turn on the oven, be sure you know how it works. If you're not certain, ask an adult to help you.

You can also roll out the clay as you would cookie dough. Cut it into tiles and press leaves and other objects into the top surface. Put the threaded end of a screw eye into the back of the tile while it is still soft and you'll be able to hang the finished product on your wall.

When hard, seal the surface with clear varnish, shellac, or liquid plastic. You can then paint your works of art with watercolors.

Gelatin

Gelatin Stalagmites

Unflavored gelatin is used by cooks to make aspics, but you can use it to make miniature stalagmites and stalactites.

Blow up a balloon, tie the opening shut, and rub the balloon on wool. You rub electrons from the wool onto the surface of the balloon to produce an area of static electricity similar to the charge you put on the phonograph record in Cereal Static Indicator.

Touch the charged area of the balloon to a dish of unflavored gelatin. The particles of gelatin are attracted by the extra electrons on the balloon just as the pieces of cereal were to the charged record.

Now raise the balloon. You'll see miniature stalagmites and stalactites of gelatin due to the static charge!

If you use flavored gelatin instead of unflavored, the bits of gelatin will fly up to the balloon somewhat like the cereal did when you brought the charged record near it.

You've probably rubbed a balloon on wool and then stuck it to a wall. The balloon was "glued" there by the attraction of the extra electrons for the neutrally charged wall.

Gelatin Gumdrops

Pour flavored gelatin dessert powder into a small dish until the gelatin is about an inch deep. Then with a medicine dropper put a drop of water in the center of the surface of the gelatin. The water is absorbed into the gelatin. Now add a second drop to the same spot. Again wait until the water disappears into the gelatin. Continue in this way until you've placed 6 drops of water on the same spot in the gelatin.

Now with a fork scoop under the spot and lift it upward. You'll find you've made a gumdrop!

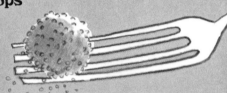

The gelatin mixed with sugar and flavoring has the unusual property of swelling and holding water in a network of protein fibers. The gumdrop you've made is actually a liquid suspended in a solid!

Commercial gumdrops are made of sugar, corn syrup, and a jellying agent such as starch, pectin, natural gum, or gelatin.

Condiments

Sugar Gems

Granulated sugar is made up of ground sugar crystals which are sold as a sweetener for baking goods, toppings, and drinks. But you can also transform them into dazzling gems!

If you haven't used a stove or handled boiling-hot liquids before, get an adult to help you dissolve 2 cups of sugar in ¾ cup of boiling water. When the solution has cooled slightly, pour it into paper cups or clear plastic glasses and set them aside where they won't be disturbed.

As the water evaporates, crystals of sugar begin to form on the bottom and sides of the container. The faster the water evaporates, the smaller the crystals will be. Be patient and allow the water to evaporate slowly and you'll get crystals the size of peas and beans in a month or so, depending on the temperature and humidity of the air above the solution.

You can buy jewelry settings at a hobby shop and attach the sugar crystals singly or in groups.

Other everyday chemicals produce different crystal shapes. In separate containers add salt, boric acid, washing soda, borax, or baking soda to hot water until no more will dissolve. Set aside to cool and before long you'll have a variety of supermarket gems.

If you want to grow large single crystals, you'll have to use special techniques which are described in books on crystals at your library.

Syrup Magnifier

While your magnifier will probably have some optical faults, it will magnify. Your friends will be surprised when they look through it and then find out you made it from syrup!

If you haven't made candy on the stove before, have an adult help you. Boil ½ cup of light corn syrup in a saucepan until a candy thermometer indicates the solution is near the "hard ball" stage, 266 degrees Fahrenheit (130 degrees Celsius).

Remove the saucepan from the heat and allow the bubbling to stop. When the solution is clear, pour it into molds with spherical hollows in them. Try measuring spoons, upside-down drinking glasses with rounded hollows in their bases, sugar or gravy spoons, ladles, and so on. Also drip a few drops of the hot solution onto a smooth surface to form drop lenses.

When the lenses have cooled and hardened, look through them at a printed page. You'll see that the more curved the lens is, the more it magnifies. You'll probably produce some "lemons," but then you can always eat them.

Corn syrup is made up of regular sugar (sucrose), and other types of sugars (especially dextrin) that retard crystallization. You can therefore heat it to hard ball without crystals forming when the solution cools.

The hardened syrup solution is somewhat like glass in that it is a stiff liquid (not a solid which by definition is made up of crystals), transparent, and bends light. While not of particular importance to a cook, these properties and the curved surfaces are what make your syrup lenses magnify.

Sugar for Marigold Odor

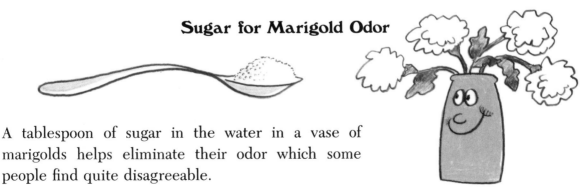

A tablespoon of sugar in the water in a vase of marigolds helps eliminate their odor which some people find quite disagreeable.

Ice-Cube Lift

With an ice cube floating in a glass of water, a piece of string, and a salt shaker nearby, challenge a friend to pick up the ice cube with the piece of string. He or she will try to loop the string around the ice cube to lift it out of the water . . . an almost impossible solution.

When your friend gives up, dip the end of the string in the water and lay it over the top surface of the ice cube. Now sprinkle salt on the string as well as the area around it. In about a minute, you can lift the ice cube right out of the water because the string will be frozen to it!

Salt lowers the freezing point of ice, causing it to melt. As the ice melts, it takes away enough heat from the water on the string to freeze the string to the ice cube.

Because salts (including those other than ordinary table salt) lower the freezing point of water, they are sprinkled on icy surfaces to melt the ice. Sidewalks and roads are cleared of ice in this way.

Salt Metal-Cleaner

Wet a cloth with vinegar and press it into salt. The mild acid of the vinegar and the sharp corners of the tiny salt crystals become a scouring powder to clean copper and brass objects.

Spice Necklace

Supermarkets carry spices because cooks use them to add flavor and aroma to foods. No one pays much attention to their appearance. But some spices are attractive and can become the beads for an unusual necklace with a nice smell.

Soak whole cloves and allspice in water for a day or two until they are soft. Using a needle threaded with nylon thread or dental floss, pierce the spices and run them onto the thread in some kind of pattern.

When completed, the spices will dry back to their original shapes and be held firmly on the thread.

Nose for Vanilla

The human nose is able to smell vanillin (the chemical in vanilla that gives the extract its characteristic odor and flavor) when there is only 1 part of vanillin to 2,000,000 parts of air!

If you're bothered by the odor of paint, add a couple of teaspoons of vanilla to the can to mask the odor.

Sauce Polish

An unknown experimenter had some brass that needed polishing—with no brass polish on hand. She (or maybe he) tried Worcestershire sauce and found it worked!

Coffee

Coffee-Filter Chemistry

Is black ink really black? Is green ink green? You'll find that there's more than meets the eye in the inks in felt-tip pens.

One way to take ink apart is to put some on a coffee filter (or a piece of paper toweling) and process it with a special technique called paper chromatography.

There are many ways to set up the apparatus. One of the simplest is to cut a strip of filter paper, put a drop of ink near one end, and allow it to dry. Then support the strip from the top of the jar or glass (see drawing). Fill the jar with enough water so that the end of the paper below the ink spot touches the water. The water is absorbed by the paper and climbs upward.

When the water reaches the spot, it dissolves the ink and carries it up the paper. As the water continues to rise, some of the components in the ink are deposited at various distances from the original spot—in effect taking the ink apart. You may be surprised at the range of colors hidden in the ink—or in water-soluble paints, food coloring . . . and even soft drinks.

Another technique that's just as simple but produces a circular pattern requires two pie plates that are slightly smaller than the filter papers. Glass plates are more fun because you can see the progress of the spreading color bands.

Flatten a pleated coffee filter, and cut a tongue ½ inch wide from the edge to near the center. At the center deposit the material to be tested. Lay the prepared filter over one plate into which you've poured the water. Bend the tongue down until it is immersed in the liquid. Cover with the other plate, turned upside down.

The simplest solvent to use is water, but not all components in the sample may dissolve in water. For this reason, other solvents can be combined with it. Try alcohol or ammonia. The library has books with chapters on chromatography if you want to go more deeply into this fascinating chemical technique.

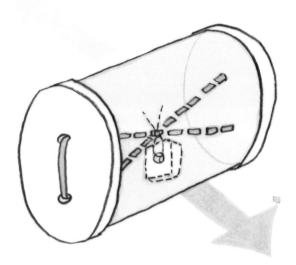

Come-Back Can

Here's an amusing toy you can make for a young friend—a coffee can the child rolls across the floor. The can stops—and then rolls back!

Cut off both ends of a coffee can. Punch two holes in two plastic lids as shown in the illustration. Thread a long rubber band through the holes in one lid and another identical rubber band through the holes in the other lid. Tie the ends of the rubber bands together inside the can with a piece of string. Then tie a weight to the string so that the weight hangs down from the rubber bands.

With the lids on the can, the part of the rubber band through the lids turns as the can rolls across the floor. The weight in the center keeps the center of the rubber band from turning. So as the can rolls, the rubber bands are twisted. Some of the energy of the push is, in effect, stored in the twisted rubber bands. When the can stops, the rubber bands unwind, rolling the can back toward its starting point.

Coffee Finger-Drip

Even though your friends will doubt you and may even be willing to bet that you can't do it, you can put your finger into a full cup of coffee until it touches the bottom of the cup without getting your finger wet!

They will suspect a trick, of course, and they will be right. Pour out a cup of dry coffee grounds from the can and dip your finger into it.

Salad Dressing

Vinegar Rocket-Launcher

The rocket is a cork with streamers attached to it with a thumbtack so you can follow its flight. The rocket launcher is a quart soda bottle containing ½ cup of water and ½ cup of vinegar.

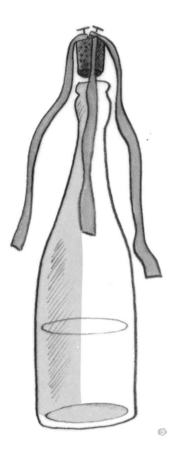

Put a teaspoon of baking soda on a 4-by-4-inch piece of paper toweling. Roll up the paper and twist the ends to keep the baking soda inside.

Outside, where you'll have plenty of altitude available, drop the paper into the bottom of the bottle and put on the cork as tightly as you can.

The liquid slowly soaks through the paper toweling. The baking soda reacts with the vinegar to produce carbon dioxide gas. As more gas forms, pressure builds up inside the bottle. You can't have an accurate countdown, so just stand back and wait. Eventually the cork shoots skyward with a loud pop!

28

Vinegar Cannon

When the vinegar rocket-launcher cork flew off, you were probably not aware of the kick of the bottle. One of the laws of motion states that for every action (popping of the cork), there is an equal and opposite reaction (the bottle is pushed in the opposite direction). To make the reaction visible, set up the rocket launcher as before; but this time put the cork in it and lay it on its side on two round pencils. As the pressure of the gas is released, the cork shoots out in one direction and the bottle recoils in the opposite direction. Some of the liquid also may spill out of the bottle, so set the cannon on an easy-to-clean surface.

This action-reaction principle is what propels rockets into outer space. The action is the hot gases coming from the rear of the rocket and the reaction is the upward motion of the rocket and its payload. Action-reaction is also used to position a space vehicle during flight. A small amount of gas is released in one direction to move the vehicle in the opposite direction.

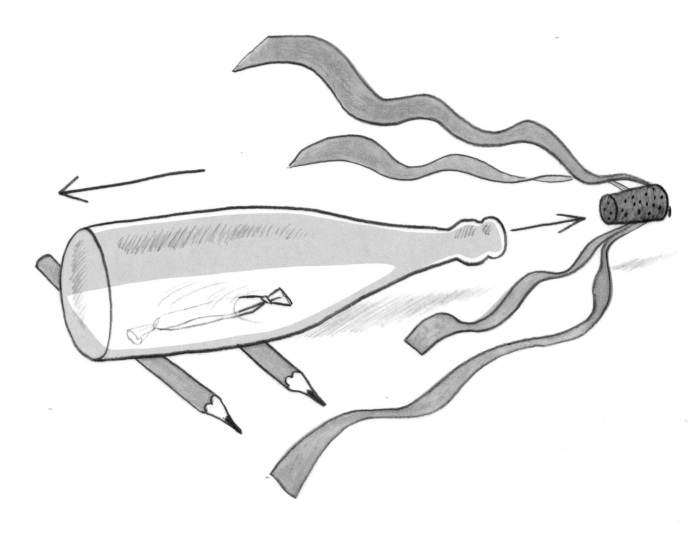

Floating Drop of Oil

Salad oil does not dissolve in water . . . as every cook knows. This property makes possible a very unusual display for your room: a large, perfectly round drop of oil floating in the center of a bottle! Guests will wonder how you managed to get a large "marble" of oil suspended in the bottle.

In addition to salad oil, you'll need water, rubbing alcohol, a large bottle, and a medicine dropper.

Practice with a small bottle or drinking glass until you've mastered the technique before floating the oil marble in a large, preferably flat-sided medicine bottle.

Pour rubbing alcohol into the bottle until it is about two-thirds full. Next pour water into it until the level of liquid almost reaches the top. The water and alcohol mix, producing a liquid that is heavier than water, but lighter than alcohol.

With the medicine dropper, slowly and carefully deposit a drop of salad oil below the surface of the liquid. To lower the drop, add water a little at a time until the drop sinks to the center of the liquid. To raise the drop, add alcohol. If you fill the container before centering the drop, simply remove some of the solution and continue adding water or alcohol until you've positioned the drop.

With the drop suspended where you want it, carefully add salad oil to it with the medicine dropper until the drop is about ¾ inch in diameter.

You can clean up any extra drops with the sharpened point of a pencil. Gently put the pencil into the solution and touch the extra drop with the pointed lead. The drop will cling to it. Move the pencil slowly to the larger drop. Touch the large drop's surface with the pencil point, transferring the smaller drop to the larger.

The oil drop forms because the oil molecules have a greater attraction for each other than for the molecules of the alcohol-water solution around them. The oil molecules at the surface of the drop are pulled inward toward the other oil molecules, forcing the oil to take the shape with the most volume for the least surface area, a sphere.

Salad-Oil Soap

Back in pioneer days, soap was made from grease and wood ashes. Today, of course, you don't make soap at home, you buy it in bars, boxes, and bottles at the supermarket.

Would you like to make some anyway—just to get an idea of how it was done? In place of grease, you can use salad oil. The wood ashes originally supplied lye, a strong chemical that reacted with the grease. You can use baking or washing soda, although they are not as active as lye. Combine ¼ cup of salad oil with ¼ cup of soda (either type) and ¼ cup of water in an enameled or glass (not metal) saucepan.

As the water boils away, the solution thickens rather suddenly. Continue to heat for several more minutes and set aside to cool.

Put a teaspoon of the concoction in a large jar, add a couple of cups of hot water, and screw on the lid. A few shakes and the jar full of suds proves that you have made your own soap.

The next step is tricky. Better get an adult to help you. He or she probably hasn't made soap either, so may find the process interesting. Simmer the ingredients in the pan over low heat to prevent spattering and possibly boiling over. Stir now and then with a wooden or plastic (not metal) spoon.

Because of the hit-or-miss method of combining and processing the ingredients, you probably shouldn't wash with your soap. Clean out the drain by pouring it down the sink!

Water-Drop Magnifier

The fact that oils and their solid cousins, waxes, do not mix with water allows you to make a simple high-powered magnifier with a drop of water as the lens.

From a roll of waxed paper, cut a square that measures a few inches on each side. Place it over the printing of a news story in a newspaper. You'll be able to read the print through the waxed paper.

Now with a medicine dropper or a plastic straw place a small drop of water on the waxed paper. Look through the drop at the newsprint. The printing you see through the drop of water is larger than the printing on each side of the drop.

Enlarge the drop slightly by adding more water. You can see more of the printing through the larger drop, but with less magnification. Put the smallest drop you can on the waxed paper. It will probably magnify so much you won't be able to see one entire letter of the printing!

A drop of water on waxed paper magnifies because it has a curved upper surface and is transparent. It bends the light reflected from the object under it in much the same manner as a glass lens of the same shape. The smaller the drop of water, the greater the curvature of the upper surface, and therefore the greater the magnification and the less area you can see.

Jar Germinator

Mayonnaise, pickles, and peanut butter come in jars with wide mouths so you can easily remove the contents. The empty jars are handy for putting in and taking out small items like nuts, bolts, nails, and screws. A wide-mouthed jar with straight sides is also ideal for making a germinator to watch seeds sprout in.

Cut paper toweling to fit the height of the jar. Line the inside of the jar with two layers of the toweling. Wet the paper to hold it in place. Pour about an inch of water in the bottom of the jar to keep the paper towels moist.

The seeds can be the ordinary edible variety (peas, beans, lentils, and so on) or those packaged for growing in the vegetable or flower garden.

Soak the seeds in water overnight to soften them and slip them between the side of the jar and the toweling about an inch or so from the top.

During the next few days, the seeds soak up more water, swell, and burst open, sending roots downward and stems and leaves upward. The food to start the growing process is contained within the seeds.

Keep records of what happened to your seeds and you can then set up controlled experiments (a science project?) to find out how light, temperature, gravity, and various materials dissolved in the water affect the growth of the seeds in your Jar Germinator.

Jar Puzzle

Here's a stunt that's been fooling people for years. Cover the mouth of a bottle with cheesecloth which obviously has many small openings in it. Pour water into the bottle through the cloth. As you turn the bottle upside down, some water will come through the cloth until you get the bottle straight up and down. Then the water stops running out!

In the past this trick was done with a milk bottle, but you can use any quart jar with a mouth no more than 2 inches across. Cover the mouth with two layers of cheesecloth held in place with a rubber band or a piece of string. Water easily goes through the holes in the cheesecloth. Why then, when you turn the jar upside down, doesn't the water flow out?

It's the invisible "skin" on water called surface tension. The tiny holes in the cheesecloth are filled with water. The combined surface tension of the hundreds of small droplets of water between the fibers of the cloth is strong enough to support the water in the jar.

In place of the cheesecloth, you can use a small square of window screen which you hold over the mouth of the bottle as you invert it. When you let go of the screen, not only is the water held up by the surface tension, but so is the screen!

Jar Terrarium

A wide-mouthed gallon jar can easily be turned into the land version of an aquarium—a terrarium. With the jar firmly positioned on its side, put in a layer of sand mixed with potting charcoal. Over this place a layer of topsoil. The "ground" section should not be any higher than the mouth of the jar. If you don't have these materials around the house and your supermarket doesn't carry them, you can find them at a nursery.

Plants for the terrarium can be any of the smaller varieties, but those that are adapted to a humid environment will probably be more likely to thrive. Try striped wintergreen, rattlesnake plantain, partridge berry, mosses of various varieties, and lichens. Nurseries often have plants especially suited for a terrarium. You can also find them for yourself in your own neighborhood or on a trip to the woods.

Once you've positioned the plants in the soil, water them thoroughly, and screw on the top of the jar. Place it in the kind of light recommended for the plants you have selected. The plants will take root and continue to grow for as long as a year . . . without your ever having to open the jar!

Dairy

Glue from Milk

If you made paste from flour, you remember it was the protein in it that did the sticking. Well, there's protein in milk, too. That's one of the reasons you drink it. Milk protein can also be made into glue.

Put 2 cups of skim milk and 6 tablespoons of vinegar into an enameled or glass saucepan and heat slowly, stirring continually. If you don't ordinarily heat milk yourself (to make hot cocoa, for instance), get an adult to help you. You can share the glue with him (or her) when you've finished making it. The milk gradually will form lumps or curdle. As soon as this begins to happen, remove the pan from the heat and continue to stir until the curdling stops. Pour the contents of the pan into a strainer to separate the solid part from the liquid.

You've just made the famous curds and whey of Little Miss Muffet fame! The solid part is the curds and the liquid is the whey. You artificially soured the milk by adding acid in the form of vinegar. A very similar method is used to form the curds that, with a little more processing, become cottage cheese. When milk sours naturally, the curdling is caused by lactic acid produced by the bacteria normally in the milk.

The more scientific name for the protein in the curds is casein, and you've probably heard of casein glue. Well, with a little more processing you can make your own.

Add ¼ cup of water and 1 level teaspoon of baking soda to the curds and stir. Many tiny bubbles form due to the chemical reaction between the baking soda and what's left of the vinegar. You now have casein glue.

Test it by pasting together two pieces of paper. If you let it dry thoroughly, you'll find that when you try to separate the sheets, the paper will tear before the paste gives way.

Carton Craft

A milk container must be waterproof to hold milk and must be rigid to be handled. Waterproof and rigid are also two of the properties of the materials necessary for building a boat . . . and you can make one for a young friend out of a milk carton with a few cuts of a knife.

Cut a milk carton across the top, down one edge, and across the bottom to the other edge. Open it up and fold the sections back to form two pontoons. The boat is finished!

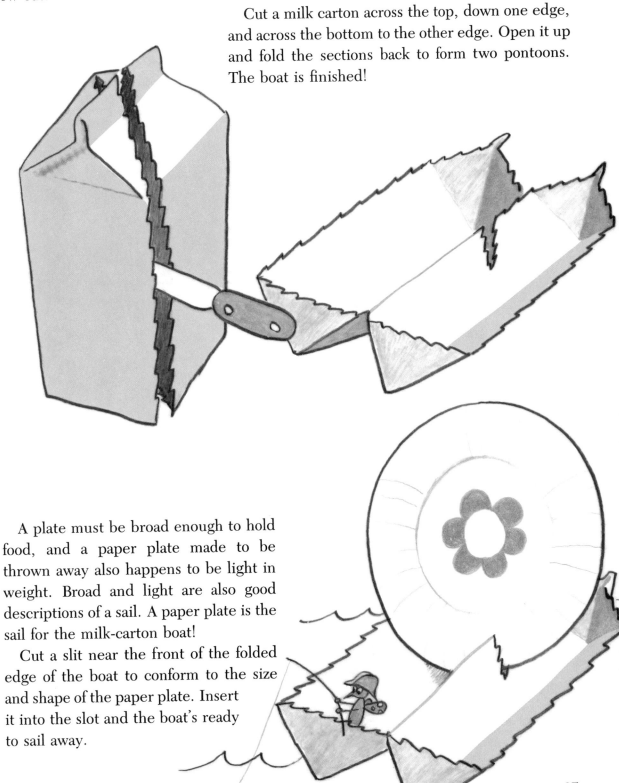

A plate must be broad enough to hold food, and a paper plate made to be thrown away also happens to be light in weight. Broad and light are also good descriptions of a sail. A paper plate is the sail for the milk-carton boat!

Cut a slit near the front of the folded edge of the boat to conform to the size and shape of the paper plate. Insert it into the slot and the boat's ready to sail away.

37

Updating the Egg-into-the-Bottle Trick

More than a hundred years ago a popular after-dinner feat was getting a hard-boiled egg into a wine decanter, in spite of the fact that the mouth of the decanter was smaller than the egg.

Years later the same trick was done with a milk bottle.

Today milk is sold in cardboard cartons—to amaze your friends, you'll have to find a bottle with the right size opening. Fortunately, one that's perfect is in the baby section of the supermarket: an 8-ounce glass nursing bottle.

A small egg just slightly larger than the mouth of the bottle works best. To have a supply of eggs for practicing, boil several of them for at least 10 minutes. If you haven't cooked things on the stove before, ask an adult to help you.

When the eggs are done, remove them from the stove and add cold water to the pan to cool them. Remove the shells. Then smear cooking oil, butter, or margarine around the mouth of the bottle.

Next you have to light a match and set a piece of paper on fire. This can be dangerous if not done carefully. Have an adult show you how to do it so you won't burn your fingers.

Accordion-fold a 4-by-4-inch piece of paper, light it, and quickly plunge it into the bottle, immediately placing the egg over the opening.

The egg starts dropping into the mouth and eventually plops to the bottom! Why?

The gases inside the bottle (both the air and the gases produced by the burning) are heated by the flame and expand. Some of the gases are forced out past the egg, which acts as a one-way valve. When the flame goes out, the gases in the bottle contract, forming a partial vacuum. The air pressure around the bottle and the egg do the rest.

Sometimes the egg is broken as it is forced into the bottle. If it's all in one piece, some wise guy is certainly going to say: "Now get the egg out of the bottle!" And it's easier to do than getting the egg into the bottle!

Fill the bottle with water. With your finger holding the egg away from the mouth, pour out the water and what's left of the burned paper. Now turn the bottle upside down so that the egg falls into the neck and blocks the opening from the inside just as it did when it was on the outside. Hold the bottle upside down and blow as hard as you can into the bottle. The air flows past the egg. When you stop blowing, the egg again acts as a one-way valve. The air pressure behind the egg slowly forces it out of the mouth and . . . plop, into your hand.

Crush an Egg in Your Hand?

You probably won't be able to do it . . . even if you squeeze with both hands! It's hard to believe that a thin, fragile egg is strong enough to withstand even a powerful pair of hands . . . until you try it.

Think of how you normally break an egg. You crack it against something hard so that the force of the blow is concentrated on a small area of the eggshell. When you squeeze an egg in your hand, the force is spread over a fairly large area of the shell. That fact alone would account for an egg's seemingly extraordinary strength.

In spite of the thinness of an eggshell, it is similar in shape to a three-dimensional arch—one of the strongest architectural forms.

When you try this stunt, be sure you don't have a ring on your finger that could concentrate the force on a small area of the shell . . . and try it over a sink or bowl—just in case!

Raw or Hard-Boiled?

When hard-boiling eggs for future use, you should mark them in some way (an ordinary pencil will do) to prevent someone from assuming they are fresh eggs. However, without breaking it, you can easily find out if an unmarked egg is raw or cooked.

Spin it on a smooth surface. A cooked egg spins easily. If stopped, it remains stopped, because it reacts to the spinning force as a solid object.

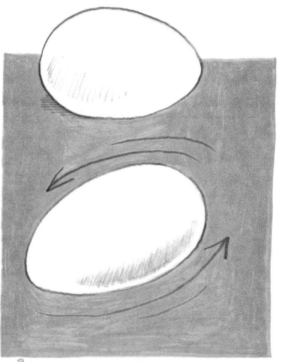

The white and yolk inside an uncooked egg, however, are fluid. The force to get it spinning must be transferred to the liquid which tends to remain at rest as the outside of the egg starts to spin. This accounts for the hesitation at the start. When stopped briefly, the fluids inside tend to continue to spin with enough force to turn the egg slightly when you take your hand away.

Engraved Gift Egg

According to one source, a riot developed back in 1808 when, by a "miracle," an egg with a message on it was found in a church. The message predicted when foreign troops would be driven out of the country. The officer in charge finally figured out how the miracle had happened and posted explanations for everyone to see. The people quieted down and began engraving their names on eggs.

Here's how to reproduce the miracle. With a china-marking pencil or wax crayon, print your friend's initials or name on the shell of a hard-boiled egg. Place the egg in a container and cover with vinegar. The tiny bubbles that form on the egg show that the acid in the vinegar is reacting with chemicals in the shell. The part of the shell under the waxy coating is protected from the action of the acid.

In an hour or two the bubbling stops, showing the acid in the vinegar has been neutralized. Replace the vinegar with a fresh supply. After about 4 hours wash off the egg under running water and gently . . . very gently . . . remove the wax from the letters with scouring powder and a soft brush. Your friend's initials will stand out in relief.

An eggshell averages about .094 of an inch (.037 of a centimeter) thick. It's composed of 3.5 percent protein, 1.5 percent water, and 95 percent mineral. The mineral (calcium carbonate) is what reacts with the acid in the vinegar. If you dissolve away half the thickness of the shell, you're handling an egg with part of its shell only about .05 of an inch thick. Sooooooo—be careful!

Meats

Fat-Spot Tester

A simple way to find out whether meat contains fat is to push it against a piece of typing or notebook paper until enough liquid is absorbed to form a spot. If the spot eventually disappears, it was mostly water, which evaporated. If the spot does not evaporate, it is fat. Try it with a piece of bacon or a hot dog. The test also works with vegetable oils.

Water and fat produce a spot on the paper by filling in the spaces between the fibers. The liquids also transmit light, conducting it right through the otherwise opaque paper. Place the paper with the spot on it over a newspaper. You can read the print through the spot!

Hold the spot up to the light. It appears much brighter than the surrounding paper. The fat (either animal or vegetable) allows some of the light falling on the back of the paper to go through it. This light, added to that already being reflected from the paper to your eyes, makes the spot appear to be brighter than the paper.

Now look at the spot with the light coming from behind you. It appears darker than the paper because some of the light falling on the spot is going through the paper, in effect being subtracted from the light being reflected to your eyes.

When the same amount of light falls on both sides of the paper, the spot disappears!

Because of this, you can use the oil spot as a simple device (a photometer) to compare the relative brightness of two light sources—two light bulbs of different wattages, for instance. In an otherwise dark room, move the paper between the two bulbs until the

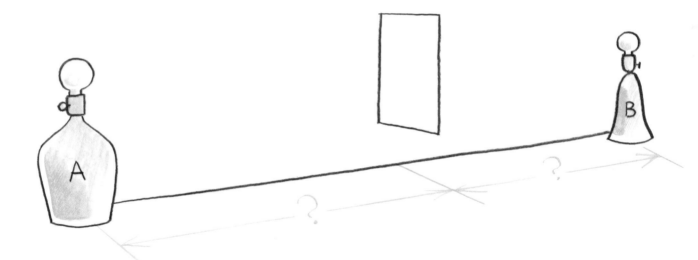

spot disappears. Measure the distance from the spot to each bulb. If bulb A is 4 feet from the paper, multiply 4 by itself (4 x 4 = 16). If bulb B is 3 feet away, multiply 3 by itself (3 x 3 = 9). Divide the larger number by the smaller: $^{16}/_9$. See the drawing. Bulb A gives off about twice as much light as bulb B.

Cleaning Supplies

Bleach Magic

Laundry bleach used to get cotton clothes whiter is a 5 percent solution of sodium hypochlorite. You can see its action by putting enough drops of ink into a glass of water (made up of hydrogen and oxygen) to color the water noticeably. The ink represents the discoloration in the clothes. As you stir, add 1 tablespoon of liquid bleach. The color disappears! The bleach released chlorine, which combined with the hydrogen in the water. The oxygen remaining combined with the coloring matter of the ink to form a colorless compound.

You can also use the bleach to remove most ink stains or ink writing. Wet the stain with vinegar first and then apply the bleach with cotton swabs.

Bleach is the hidden gimmick for a simple magic trick. A small amount of bleach in the bottom of an empty glass will be unnoticed. Add red food coloring to water in an identical glass until you have an appropriate wine color. A few minutes after you pour the "wine" into the "empty" glass, it changes to water! You'll have to experiment with the number of drops of food coloring you'll need to make the water look like wine and how much bleach you'll need to remove the color.

Obviously no one should drink the "wine" or "water" because they are only props and not the real things.

Bleach Art

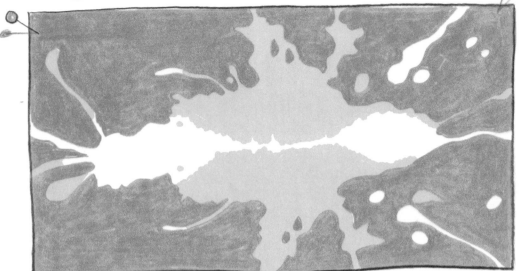

Laundry bleach removes unwanted color from clothes. It also removes color from other materials and can be the medium for some interesting effects.

The colors of construction paper quickly disappear with the application of bleach. The trick is to apply and spread bleach in a manner that will result in an artistic or at least unusual pattern. Experiment applying the bleach with a spoon, brush, swab, and so on. Spread it around on the paper by blowing (perhaps through a straw to direct the force of the air), tilting, and folding. You'll be able to see the patterns almost immediately. All the color in the paper will be gone within a minute. When you have produced a work of art, allow it to dry before hanging it on your wall or giving it to a friend.

Bleach Oxidizer

You can prove that oxygen is liberated by bleach by putting two small steel-wool balls of equal size in two glasses. Cover the balls with equal amounts of water. To one glass add a tablespoon of vinegar. To the other add a tablespoon of vinegar and one of bleach.

After half an hour, the steel wool in the glass without the bleach is unchanged, while the ball in the glass with the bleach is very rusty. Rust is iron that has combined with oxygen in the presence of water.

Soap Tricks

One of the reasons soaps and detergents clean is that they break the surface tension of water. This is an invisible skinlike quality due to the packing together of molecules at the surface of water.

Sprinkle pepper or talcum powder on the surface of cold, clean water in a shallow dish. The particles spread out and cover the surface. Now touch a bit of soap or put a drop of liquid soap or detergent at the side of the dish. As the soap or detergent dissolves, it breaks the surface tension in that area. The tension on the rest of the surface pulls the floating particles to the side opposite the soap. Pour out the water and rinse out the container to get rid of the soap before trying another surface-tension trick.

Float a loop of string in the middle of the surface of the water. Touch soap to the water or put a drop of liquid soap or detergent inside the loop. The string is pulled outward by the surface tension around it to form a circle.

Fairly large objects float on water if the surface tension is not broken. Try a paper clip lowered onto the water with a fork. A plastic berry basket is also very impressive floating on the water in spite of all the holes in the bottom. A needle has been a long-time favorite floater. All of these items sink to the bottom when you touch soap or detergent to the water surface.

Paper boats with a small slot at the back are propelled across the water if you put a bit of soap or detergent in the water at the forward end of the slot. Cutting the slot to one side propels the boat in a circle.

A paper spiral with a bit of soap or detergent in the water in the center spins as a result of the breaking of the surface tension of the water along the inner areas of the spiral.

Uses for Soap

To pick up small beads that have fallen to the floor, lightly rub a dampened bar of soap over the area. The beads stick to the soap. Invisible pieces of broken glass can be picked up in the same way. With a knife, scrape the surface of the soap with the glass in it onto a piece of paper and discard it. Before you use the soap again, be sure there are no bits of glass left in it.

Soap has been used as a lubricant for a long time. It is especially good for making drawers slide freely. Nails and screws will go into wood more easily if they are first rubbed on a bar of soap.

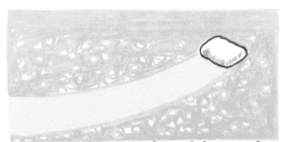

Coating the inside of the cap of a bottle of glue or nail polish with soap will keep the cap from sticking.

A thin sliver of soap can be used to mark cloth for sewing. It can be brushed off or washed away when the garment has been completed.

Soapy water is the standard solution for detecting leaks in air mattresses, tires, and other inflatables. The bubbles quickly pinpoint the leak.

Coat the underside of a pan with soap before heating it over an open fire at a campground. The soot collects on the soapy surface, and you can easily remove both the soap and the soot in the wash water.

Decorations for a festive occasion can be fashioned out of a cupful of soap flakes or liquid soap to which you have added a little water. Whip the solution until it's thick and stiff like whipped cream. With it you can paint pictures or write messages on windows and mirrors. Add sequins, beads, or cookie decorations for an artistic touch.

Giant Bubbles

You can blow bubbles several feet in diameter with a mixture of liquid soap or detergent, glycerin, and water. The glycerin is the secret ingredient that adds strength to the bubble solution. Mix together 1 part soap or detergent with 1 part glycerin and 6 parts distilled water. Pour into a large tray or cookie sheet.

Form a 12-inch circle with a handle. out of stiff wire about the diameter of coat-hanger wire. You can try an actual coat hanger, but they are often coated to prevent rusting. The coating prevents the bubble solution from clinging to the wire.

Dip the wire circle into the bubble solution and bring it out at an angle so that a film of solution fills the inside of the circle. Now sweep the wire through the air to form a large bubble. A twist at the end of the sweep helps disengage the bubble from the wire.

A bubble (small or large) is really three bubbles in one. There's an outside layer of water, a middle layer of soap (and in this case glycerin), and an inner layer of water.

When large bubbles like these break, they leave considerable soap behind, which can mess up a kitchen floor. Be prepared to wipe it up (cleaning the floor at the same time), or blow the bubbles outside.

48

Soap Defogger

The fact that soap breaks up the surface tension of water is the reason it keeps windows or mirrors from becoming fogged up with steam. Wipe a window or mirror with a damp cloth with a small amount of liquid soap or detergent on it. The very thin film on the glass is not visible, but prevents the water from forming into the tiny drops that obscure the view.

You can use this fact to perform a simple magic trick. Put a drop or two of liquid soap or detergent into a cup of water. Dip the tip of your finger (or better yet a cotton swab) into the solution and write the number 5 on a mirror or window. The film should be thin enough to be invisible.

Now ask a friend to choose a number, add the next higher number to it, add 9 to the result, divide by 2, and subtract the original number. Breathe on the invisible number you have written on the glass. The answer stands out as the area around it becomes foggy. Regardless of what number your friend starts with, the answer is always 5.

If your windows fog up on cold days, you can write your name or a message on them with a soap solution. Your writing stands out because it remains clear as the rest of the window becomes foggy. You can also write a message on a bathroom mirror that fogs up when someone takes a shower. As a member of your family steps out of the shower, he or she is greeted by your message.

49

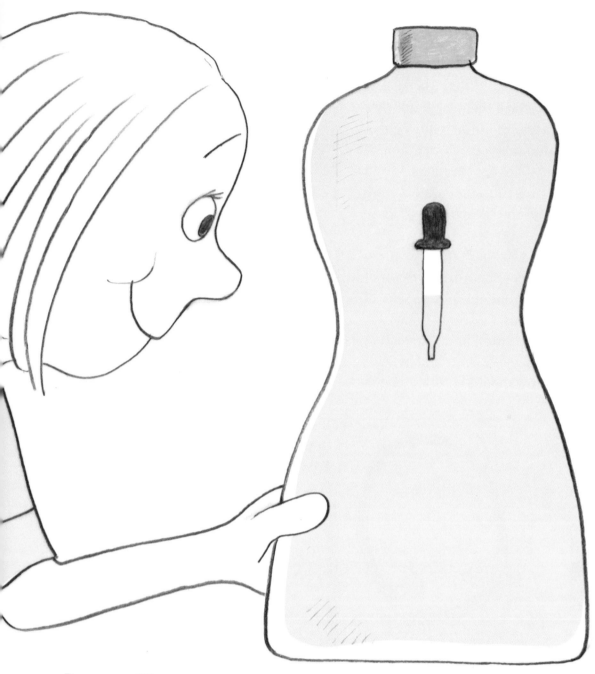

Dropper Diver

You hold in your hand a clear plastic bottle filled with water. Floating at the top of the bottle is an ordinary medicine dropper. At your command the dropper sinks to the bottom of the bottle. Another command, and it rises to the top. To anyone not in the know, the dropper seems to hear and follow what you're saying!

The mysterious dropper diver is easy to make out of a clear, quart-sized plastic bottle. You'll probably find one filled with liquid soap in the cleaning section of your supermarket. Be sure to rinse it out thoroughly to get rid of all the soap. Then fill it almost to the top with water.

Put a medicine dropper into a glass of water to make sure that it floats. Then squeeze the bulb end to draw water up into the dropper. If it still floats, add more water. Keep adding (or subtracting) water until you get the dropper to just barely float upright in the water. Then carefully (so as not to lose any of the water in it) transfer the dropper to the bottle.

Fill the bottle to the very top with water and make sure there are no air bubbles trapped inside the bottle before you screw on the top.

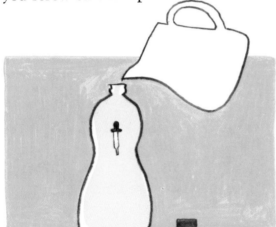

Gently squeeze the bottle. The pressure you put on the sides of the bottle is transferred to the water inside— including the water inside the dropper. You can see the level of the water in the dropper go up as you squeeze the bottle. As the water level inside the dropper rises, it squeezes the air above it into a smaller space. The dropper-air-water combination becomes less buoyant and the dropper sinks.

Release the pressure on the bottle. The water level inside the dropper falls and the air expands. The dropper is now as buoyant as when you started, so it rises.

When you have the dropper buoyancy properly adjusted, with a bit of practice you can make the dropper follow your finger up and down the outside of the bottle by adjusting the pressure of your finger!

Many versions of this Cartesian diver have been constructed over the years. It was named after René Descartes (1596–1650), a great French scientist and philosopher who invented coordinate geometry and made major contributions to the philosophy of science.

Ammonia Fountain

The bottle of ammonia on the supermarket shelf is water with ammonia gas dissolved in it. And it's amazing how much ammonia gas, water can hold. At 60 degrees Fahrenheit (15 degrees Celsius) it will absorb 683 times its own volume of the gas. When heated to 80 degrees Fahrenheit (26 degrees Celsius), it can absorb only 29 percent of its volume of the gas. The bottled ammonia gas in the store is at room temperature. Heated to 80 degrees, the ammonia gas comes out of the solution. You can smell it (it's the odor of smelling salts) and use it to make a miniature fountain.

To drive out the ammonia gas, you have to heat some ammonia water in a saucepan. If you're not familiar with the workings of the stove, ask an adult to help you. Collect some of the gas in a baby's nursing bottle with a funnel as shown. Then screw on the cap with the nipple upside down. Hold the top of the bottle in a bowl or pan of cold water.

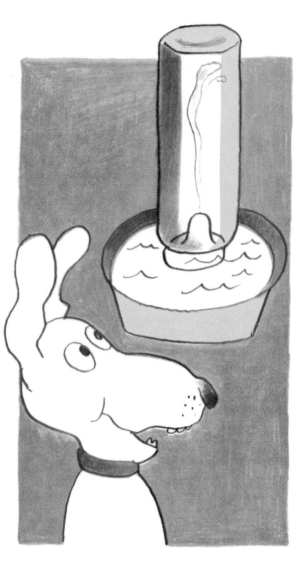

With your finger, push up the nipple to get a little water into the bottle through the hole in the nipple. Some of the ammonia gas in the bottle dissolves in the water, lowering the pressure inside the bottle. Air pressure forces water to flow up through the hole in the nipple and more ammonia dissolves in it. Depending on the size of the hole and the amount of ammonia gas in the bottle, the stream of water entering through the hole in the nipple can squirt with surprising force all the way to the other end of the bottle!

Broom Trick

The springiness of the bristles of a broom is what makes sweeping the floor possible. The springiness is also the secret of how to accomplish what looks like an impossible challenge.

Set up a glass, pie plate, plastic sponge, and ball as shown. The challenge is to get the ball into the glass using only the broom to touch any of the items.

You can do it with a flair by putting your foot on the bristles of the broom, pulling back on the handle, and letting go. The handle hits the edge of the pie plate that's beyond the edge of the table. As it is sent flying, the rim of the pie plate knocks the sponge out of the way, and the ball falls neatly into the glass. If you want to add an extra element of suspense, substitute a hard-boiled egg for the ball.

The ball and glass remain where they are instead of moving with the pie plate because of inertia, the tendency of a mass to stay at rest unless a force is applied to it. The force you apply to the broom is transferred to the pie plate and the sponge but not to the ball or glass. The ball is at rest above the glass because it is supported against the force of gravity by the sponge and the pie plate. As soon as they are out of the way, the ball is pulled downward into the glass.

Broom Pushover

A broom with a stiff wooden handle can give you superhuman strength.

Challenge a friend to push you over with a broom held at arm's length as shown. Hold the center of the broom with one hand, so that your friend has to push slightly upward. Then, as he pushes forward, push up. The leverage involved gives you so much mechanical advantage, you can't be pushed over!

Clothespin Clamp

Clothespins are clamps to hold the wash on the line, but their clamping action has been put to many other uses: holding notes, keeping small parts in place for gluing or soldering, and so on.

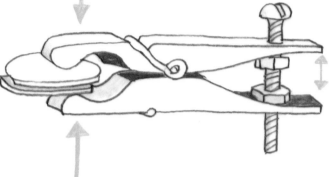

If the force of the spring that keeps the clothespin closed is not strong enough for the clamping job, drill holes in the ends, and add a bolt and two nuts, as shown. By turning the nuts to apply pressure on the insides of the ends, you can increase the force of the clamping action at the other end.

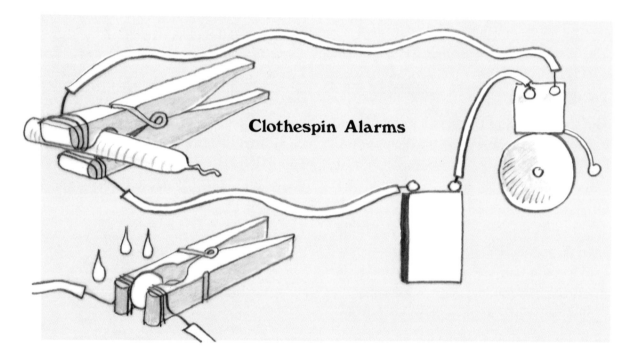

Clothespin Alarms

You can use the clamping action of a clothespin to make a homemade fire alarm. Wind one bared wire around each jaw of a clothespin, making it into a switch. Attach the other ends of the wires to a dry cell and a bell, and connect the dry cell and the bell to each other, as shown. Keep the clothespin jaws apart with something that will melt in the heat of a fire: a piece of candle, paraffin, or candy.

You can adapt the same setup to a rain alarm. Keep the jaws apart with something that will dissolve in the rain: a lump of sugar, a baby aspirin, or a vitamin C tablet.

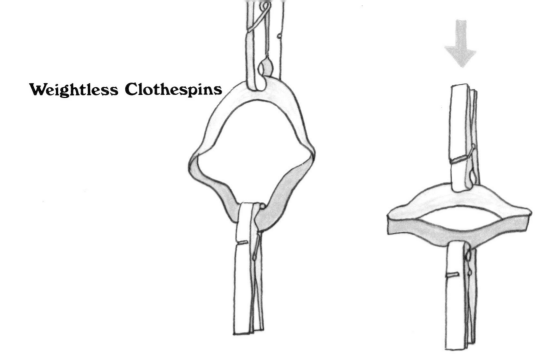

Weightless Clothespins

With nothing more than two clothespins and a large rubber band you can prove that as they fall objects (including astronauts) are weightless.

Attach clothespins to the sides of a large, thick rubber band. Hold up one clothespin. The weight of the lower clothespin pulls the sides of the rubber band apart.

Now drop the clothespins. You'll see that as the rubber band falls, its two sides come together.

Weight is a measurement of the effect of the force of gravity. As an object falls, gravity acts on it, moving it toward the earth. But think of the rubber band as a spring scale weighing the lower clothespin before you dropped it. As the rubber-band scale falls, it contracts, showing the lower clothespin has no weight to pull the two sides of the rubber band apart. If the lower clothespin is weightless, then you can assume that the upper clothespin and the rubber band (and astronauts) also are weightless as they fall.

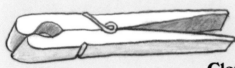

Clothespin Wedge

A clothespin is a handy wedge. Just as it comes from the store, it's a thick wedge. Take it apart and each of the legs is a thinner wedge to hold open a door, prop up a table or chair with one leg too short, and so on.

Sponge Garden

Because a sponge holds water in its many small cavities, it's an ideal surface on which to grow seeds.

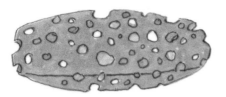

Soak the sponge and place it in a shallow dish of water. Sprinkle seeds over the top surface of the sponge. Try the seeds of grasses, sweet alyssum, coleus, and any other small seeds you may have left over from planting a garden. The shoots of almost any plant make an attractive display.

Be sure to keep water in the dish so that the sponge never has a chance to dry out. Of course as soon as leaves appear, the food stored in the seeds will have been used up. Add liquid plant food to the water to supply nutrients. You may be surprised at how tall your sponge garden grows!

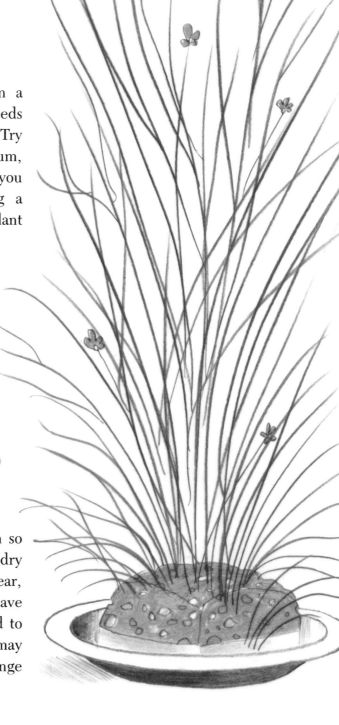

Mothball Frost

Put a mothball or a teaspoon of moth flakes into a large jar and screw on the lid. Place the jar in a saucepan of water and heat it until the mothball melts. Remove the jar from the heat. Beautiful, delicate crystals of mothball frost form inside the jar!

Mothballs and moth flakes are made of a solid that at room temperature changes to a vapor in much the same way that heated water gives off water vapor—the white mist that most people call steam. Because mothballs and moth flakes change directly from a solid to an invisible vapor, they slowly get smaller and eventually disappear (a process called sublimation). The vapor is what repels moths.

As you raise the temperature of the mothball above that of the room, it melts to a liquid which can change to a vapor more quickly. When the vapor comes into contact with the sides of the jar, it's cooled and changes back to a solid again in the form of delicate crystals that look like frost. Similar crystals were pressed together to form the solid mothballs or moth flakes you started with.

Cookware

Rolling-Pin Secret Code

You ordinarily use a rolling pin for pressing dough into a thin sheet, but you can also use it as the key for a code with which you can send secret messages to a friend.

Cut 1-inch strips from a sheet of typing paper and paste them together end to end to form one long strip. Adding-machine paper cut into a strip 1 inch wide will also work. Tape one end to the surface of the rolling pin near the handle.

Wind the strip around the rolling pin to form a spiral with the edges of the strip touching each other. Continue winding the strip until you come to the other end of the rolling pin. Cut off the rest of the paper and tape the end of the strip to the rolling pin.

Now write your secret message along the length of the rolling pin so that each of the letters in the message is on a different section of the spiral. When you unwind the strip, the letters will be out of order and the message unreadable.

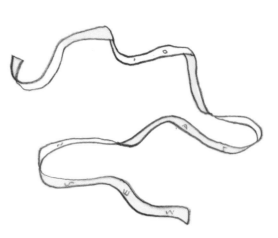

All your friend has to do is wind the strip around an identical rolling pin. The letters on the strip will again be lined up . . . and your secret message will be readable.

No other-size cylinder will enable your friend to decipher the message because a cylinder of another diameter will line up the letters in a different order.

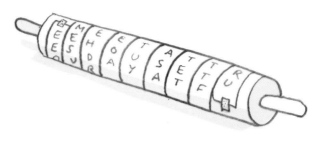

Of course, you don't have to use a rolling pin if you have another cylinder handy. A piece of pipe, a wooden dowel, a tall tin can, a pencil, or any other cylindrical object will work as long as both you and your friend have the same-size cylinder.

Before the birth of Christ, a similar cylinder-type code was supposed to have been used by officers in the Greek army to send secret messages to each other.

Funnel Stethoscope

A funnel is shaped like a cone so you can pour liquids into a container with a small mouth. Because of its shape, you can also use a funnel to hear your heart beat.

Fit a length of rubber tubing over the spout of a funnel. Hold the other end of the tubing to your ear and place the funnel over your heart. You'll be able to hear it beating!

If you don't hear it right away, don't worry. You have a heart! But you may not be sure exactly where it is. It's not on the left side of your chest as some people assume, but very near the middle. In fact, you can use the funnel stethoscope to locate your heart by moving it around on your chest until the beat is loudest.

You can also listen to someone else's heart by holding the funnel to his or her chest.

Doctors use a more sophisticated version of the funnel and tube to listen to a patient's heart. To the doctor's practiced ear, the sounds heard through the stethoscope indicate the condition of the patient's heart.

Funnels Roll "Uphill"

You can make a "gravity-defying" device out of two large funnels taped together as shown. With two yardsticks and books of different thicknesses, form a track that's lower and narrower at one end than the other. After a little adjustment of the space between the two tracks (to accommodate the size of the funnels), place the funnels at the lower end. They roll "uphill" toward the higher end!

Actually they don't roll upward at all. If you look at the system from one side, you'll see that the center of the funnels (looking directly into one of the spouts) actually goes down as they roll.

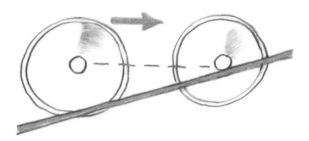

The illusion works because the sides of the funnels slope upward, allowing the center of the funnels to go down while the track goes up.

Aluminum Silver Cleaner

Cleaning silverware is a tedious job . . . but not when you use aluminum to do it.

To see how efficiently aluminum cleans silver, tarnish some silverware artificially by placing it in dishes of mustard, mayonnaise, or soft-boiled egg. Varying amounts of tarnish will form on the silver in 6 hours or so.

The tarnish is silver sulfide, formed by the chemical reaction between the silver and the sulfur in the foods. Similar but less severe darkening appears on silver that has been exposed to such sulfur-containing foods or their vapors.

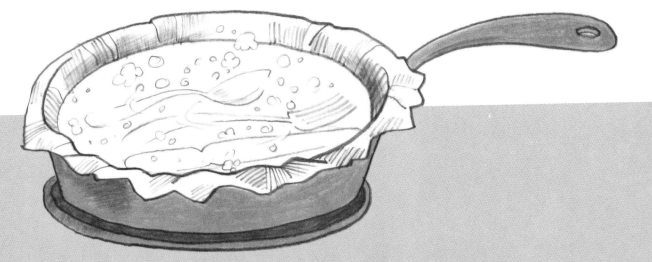

To remove the tarnish, line the inside of a large pot with aluminum foil and add water with a measuring cup until the pot is half-full. To every quart of water you've put into the pot, add 1 teaspoonful of baking soda and 1 teaspoonful of salt. Heat the solution until it begins to boil. Place the tarnished silver in the solution, making sure that each piece touches the foil. Keep the solution boiling gently until the tarnish disappears.

You actually have made a form of electric battery. The aluminum in the foil is the negative pole and the silver, the positive. The hot liquid is a chemically active solution called an electrolyte. The silver-sulfide tarnish goes into the solution and is broken apart. A feeble electric current deposits the silver back onto the silverware. The sulfur combines with some of the chemicals in the solution and is deposited onto the foil. You have, in effect, transferred the tarnish from the silver to the aluminum foil with electricity. When the silver is clean, rinse it in fresh water and wipe it dry.

Water Beads

Heat up a large frying pan and sprinkle a couple of drops of water into it. When the temperature is right, they will roll around as though they were beads!

The bottom surface of the water drops is heated to boiling and forms an invisible layer of steam that keeps the water drops from actually touching the metal of the frying pan. The drops roll around on this layer of steam.

If the pan is too hot, the drops quickly boil away. If the pan is not hot enough, the steam forms too slowly and the drops spread out and again boil away. When the temperature is just right, the drops roll around for quite a while slowly getting smaller, and finally disappearing.

You may have seen someone wet his (or more likely her) finger and "touch" the bottom of an iron to see if it is hot enough to begin ironing. It's the layer of steam formed from the water on the finger that makes the "psst" sound and keeps the finger from actually touching the hot metal.

Double-Boiler Rain

A glass double boiler is a convenient apparatus for showing what makes it rain.

Put water in the lower section and plenty of water and ice cubes in the upper section. Heat the water in the lower section to a boil. The steam coming from the boiling water is cooled by the cold surfaces of the upper section. The steam changes back to water which collects in drops. As the drops get bigger (and heavier) they fall down into the water as "rain."

The boiling water represents the surface of water heated by the sun. The steam is the water that evaporates into the air as water vapor. As the vapor rises, it's cooled. When conditions are right, droplets form which you see as clouds. As the droplets collect more moisture, they finally become heavy enough to fall back to the earth as rain.

Juices

Juice-Can Feeder

A large juice can, two aluminum pie plates, and a piece of coat-hanger wire can be fashioned into a gravity bird feeder that automatically supplies new seeds as the birds consume the supply "on deck."

Punch a hole in the bottom of the juice can and with an opener make a series of holes around the base. Punch holes in the centers of the pie plates and through them thread a length of coat-hanger wire. Form a circle at the bottom of the wire on which the lower pie plate can rest firmly.

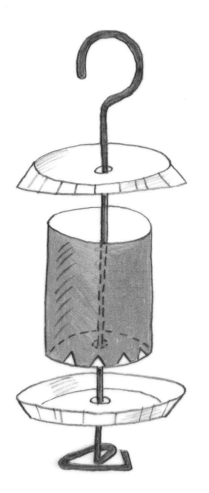

Fill the can with birdseed and hang it from a branch of a tree located so that you can watch the action out a window.

The top pie plate keeps out the rain. The bottom tray holds the seeds and is a perch for the birds to sit on as they help themselves.

As the birds eat the seeds on the pie plate and from the holes in the base of the can, gravity will supply more seeds until the can is empty.

Juice-Can Charcoal Starter

Starting a barbecue with charcoal as the fuel is a time-consuming chore . . . and can be dangerous if you use starter fluid. The next time your family has a barbecue, you can show them how to speed up the process with a large juice can. If you're not experienced in the use of matches, ask one of the adults present to give you a hand.

Remove both ends of the can and set it in the center of the grill basin. Crumple up several sheets of newspaper and stuff them into the bottom section of the can. Light the paper and, when it has been burning for a few seconds, toss lumps of charcoal into the can a couple at a time, until you've got enough for the cooking at hand.

The heat of the burning paper ignites the lumps of charcoal with ease. They'll be burning at full strength in a few minutes. With a pair of pliers or tongs, lift up the can so the charcoal falls out the bottom. Be careful where you put the can, because it is still *hot!*

Picnic Supplies

Straw Oboe

A soda straw is a thin tube with air in it. The fact that it's cuttable means you can make it into an oboe.

Pinch one end flat and cut off the corners to form two little reeds. Hold the

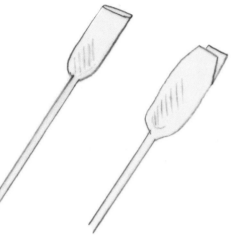

reeds in your mouth without squeezing them or letting your teeth or tongue touch them. Now blow hard.

If no sound is produced, either the reeds are open too far (pinch them closer together with your lips), or they're closed (open them slightly with your lips). Eventually you'll make a sound something like that of an oboe, which also has two reeds, but out of wood.

The two reeds opening and closing at high speed first allow air to flow into the straw and then stop the flow. The vibrating air is what produces the sound.

The length of the air column deter-

mines the pitch. Cut pieces off the bottom end of the straw as you blow. You'll hear a higher note. With practice, you should be able to play the scale, upward of course. Carefully cut small holes along the length of the straw about an inch or so apart. Cover them with your fingers. You can play simple tunes by covering and uncovering the holes as you blow your straw oboe.

Straw Through Potato

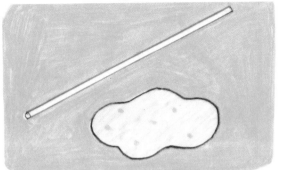

Plunge a soda straw through a raw baking potato? Impossible, your friends will say. Yet when you know the secret, you can do it!

The trick is to jab the straw at the potato with as much force as you can and at right angles to the surface of the potato.

Get a good grip on the straw by pinching one end between your thumb and first finger. Then plunge the straw straight down toward the potato. You probably won't hit it exactly right the first time. Try again with a new straw and eventually you'll get the right combination of force and angle.

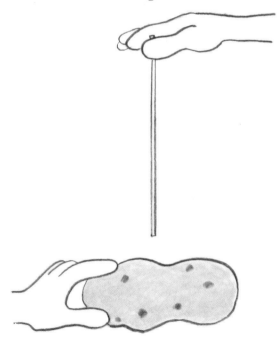

Most people think of a straw as a relatively weak tube that is easily bent. They don't realize that a straw has considerable strength when a push or pull is applied along its length.

When you hit the surface of a potato with a straw at a right angle, the straw does not bend. Instead, it goes clear through the potato.

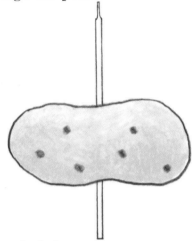

Fresh baking potatoes are easiest to pierce. Older potatoes have lost some of their moisture and therefore have tougher skins. If older potatoes are all you have, soak them in water for an hour or so before trying this stunt.

Paper straws are most spectacular, but they're hard to find these days. Plastic straws are stiffer but by no means easy to plunge through a potato. If you're going to do this at a special affair where you want to be sure of the outcome, buy several baking potatoes and practice.

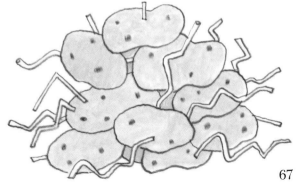

Straw Pickup

Challenge your friends to pick up an empty bottle with a soda straw without touching the outside of the bottle. Try as they might, the straw seems too weak to support the bottle.

You pick up the bottle by using the soda straw's hidden strength.

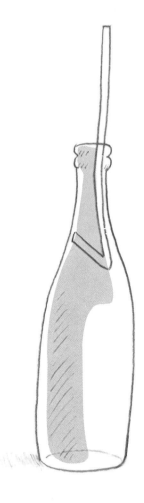

If you plunged a straw through a potato, you know that a straw is surprisingly strong when a push or pull is applied along its length.

After your friends give up, simply bend the end of the straw, forming a section wider than the mouth of the bottle. Now slip the bent end into the bottle and maneuver it so the end is wedged against the inside of the bottle. Using the strength of the straw to withstand a push (on the shorter section inside the bottle) and a pull (on the longer section you're holding), you can lift the bottle by the straw with no trouble at all.

Paper-Plate Illusion

With a paper plate and a pair of scissors, you can make an amazing optical illusion right in front of your friends. In spite of the fact that they saw you make it, they'll find it hard to believe their eyes.

Cut half the rim off the paper plate. Then cut the half-rim in two so you can lay one half over the other.

Trim the edges of both pieces at the same time to make sure they are exactly the same length.

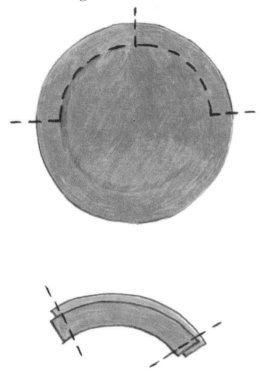

Now hold one above the other, lining up one of the edges as shown in the drawing. The bottom piece looks much longer than the top one in spite of the fact that your friends saw you cut them out at the same time!

Reverse their positions. The one that was on top and looked shorter now is on the bottom and looks longer!

Why? Your friends unconsciously compare the shorter bottom arc of the top piece with the longer upper arc of the bottom piece. No matter which piece is on the bottom, it always looks longer.

Hold the pieces in various positions. The optical illusion continues until you turn the bottom piece upside down. Now the shorter arcs are next to each other and the pieces look the same length.

Paper-Plate Puzzle

If you cut a one-quarter slice out of a paper plate, set the plate on a table, and roll a marble around the plate's rim, in which direction will the marble go when it gets to the cut edge? Will it continue to curve inward, go straight ahead, or curve outward?

The action of the marble follows Newton's first law of motion: a body in motion will continue in a straight line unless a force is applied to it to move it out of the straight line. When you give the marble a push, it would roll in a straight line, but the curved edge of the paper plate supplies the force to push it into a circular path. As soon as the push is removed, the marble rolls in a straight line.

Paper-Plate Sailer

A paper plate is shaped something like a Frisbee. Toss a paper plate with a twisting motion to get it spinning, and you can sail it through the air.

You may have to paste two thin plates together to keep them from bending and some plates are shaped better for sailers than others. With the right kind of plate and a bit of practice, you can get some spectacular trajectories.

At one time a vaudeville act entertained audiences with its fantastic paper-plate-throwing abilities.

Dribble Glass

Fill a plastic glass by plunging it under the surface of water in a container. When you turn the glass upside down and raise it almost all the way out of the water, the water stays in the glass well above the level of the water in the container. It's one of the simplest scientific tricks that anyone can do, until your friends try it.

When they raise the glass, the water in it slowly sinks until it is at the same level as the water in the container!

Why can you do it and they can't?

The water stays in the glass because the weight of the air (air pressure) on the surface of the water in the container is greater than the weight of the water in the glass. If air can get into the glass, the air pressure causes the level of the water to drop. How can air get into the glass? Because your glass has a tiny hole near the bottom made with a small hot nail!

To get the nail hot enough to melt through the plastic, hold the nail with a pair of pliers in the flame of a candle or over the stove. If you're not sure you can do it safely, get an adult to make the hole for you.

When you do the trick, you hold a thumb or finger over the hole. When your friends try it, they're unaware of the hole that allows the air to push the water out of the glass.

The reason it's called a dribble glass is that you can cover the hole with a finger and fill the glass with water in the ordinary way. Then hand the glass to a friend. Be sure you know him well enough to tell what his reaction will be when the water dribbles over him out of the hole.

Plastic-Glass Phone

This is an up-to-date version of a toy that children have made for a long time out of tin cans and paper cups. Clear plastic glasses work better than tin cans and are sturdier than paper cups.

First melt a hole in the bottom of two large clear plastic glasses. If you read about how to make the dribble glass, you know that you hold a small nail with a pair of pliers in the flame of a candle or over the stove. If you're not sure you can do it safely, get an adult to make the holes for you.

Thread the end of a long string through one of the holes and tie a bulky knot so the string can't be pulled back out of the hole.

Have a friend take the glass into another room, trailing the thread behind her. When she's far enough away (and the thread is still in a straight line), thread your end through your glass, tie a large knot, and pull the thread between you until it is stretched straight.

When you talk into the glass, its bottom vibrates. The vibrations travel down the length of the string and vibrate the bottom of your friend's glass. By putting her glass up to her ear, she'll be able to hear you quite distinctly.

When you say "Over," you're telling her you're through talking and it's her turn to speak into her glass, while you listen with yours.

If you try to turn a corner and the thread between the two phones touches a solid (the frame of a door, for instance), the vibrations traveling down the thread are stopped. However, with a little preparation, you *can* turn the corner. To the telephone line tie a short piece of thread, attaching its other end to the side of the doorframe to keep the line away from the corner. Now the vibrations can continue down the thread and reach the other end.

Paper-Cup Puzzle

Challenge your friends to measure out 4 ounces of water using only a 3-ounce cup and a 5-ounce cup. They can work out the puzzle on paper, but doing it with actual cups and water is probably more fun (though messier).

With a measuring cup, put 3 ounces of water into a paper cup, mark the level, and cut it off so that it holds only 3 ounces and no more. Do the same with another paper cup, cut off at 5 ounces. Now you're ready to see how logical your friends are. Can they use the two cups to measure out 4 ounces of water?

Here's what they'll have to do: Fill the 3-ounce cup with water and pour it into the 5-ounce cup. Then fill the 3-ounce cup again and pour water into the 5-ounce cup until it is full. An ounce of water is left in the 3-ounce cup. Empty the 5-ounce cup and pour in the ounce of water from the smaller cup. Now fill the 3-ounce cup again.

Pour the 3 ounces of water into the larger cup. It now holds 4 ounces of water.

Paper-Cup Flowerpots

Paper cups are waterproof and easily crushed and torn, which makes them excellent containers in which to start seeds.

Punch holes around the bottom for drainage, fill with potting soil, and plant the seeds according to the instructions on the package. When a seedling is ready to be transplanted, cut or tear away the paper cup. Without disturbing its roots, you can place the new plant in a hole in the ground.

73

Paper Towels

Paper-Tube Kazoo

The next time a roll of paper towels, toilet tissue, or aluminum foil has been used up, don't throw away the paper tube. Instead make a kazoo that you can hum into and make a pleasant, buzzy sound.

Cut out a piece of waxed paper or tissue paper big enough to go over the end of the tube. Hold it in place with a rubber band. Punch a hole in the side of the tube with a pencil. That's all there is to it.

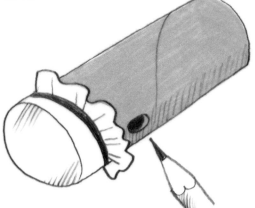

With the open end of the tube near your mouth, hum or sing into the tube. The paper at the other end vibrates, producing the peculiar kazoo sound.

Tube X-Ray

Hold a cardboard tube up to one eye and hold your hand alongside it. Keep both eyes open. You see your hand with a hole in it!

Naturally, you're not seeing through your hand. Your brain combines the images from both your eyes which ordinarily are focused on the same object or scene. In this case, one eye sees your hand and the other the hole in the tube. Your brain combines them to produce the "hole" in your hand.

Tube Puzzle

Take a good look at the paper tube inside a roll of paper toweling. It's glued together in a spiral fashion. What was the shape of the piece of cardboard before it was twisted into a tube?

You may not know the name of the geometric figure, so draw it on a piece of paper. Then open up the tube to see if you were correct. The plane figure represented by the open tube is called a parallelogram because the opposite sides are parallel to each other.

Baby Supplies

Nipple Expansion

The nipple on a baby's nursing bottle is made of rubber, so you expect it to expand—but not enough to hold 9 ounces of a carbonated drink! You won't believe it until you try it!

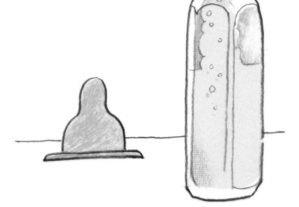

In the baby section find a nipple without a hole in it. (Mother is supposed to make her own hole.) You may have to get a hole-less nipple at a drugstore, but blowing it up with soda is worth the extra trip. Pour carbonated soft drink into an 8-ounce glass baby bottle which holds about 9 ounces when you fill it to the top. Screw on the cap with the nipple in it as quickly as you can in order to lose as little of the gas bubbling out of the soda as possible.

With the cap on tightly, gently rock the bottle back and forth. The agitation forces the carbon dioxide gas out of the solution. Gradually the gas inflates the nipple. Eventually it expands enough so that when you hold the bottle upside down, the nipple holds the entire 9 ounces of liquid—with room to spare!

Tableware

Muscle-Tester

Hold a table knife with the blade parallel to the top of a table preferably covered with a tablecloth. Don't allow your hand or arm to touch the table. Now place a hairpin on the edge of the knife so that its feet just touch the table and it leans forward toward the tip of the knife. Even though you hold your hand as steady as you can, the hairpin "walks" down the knife and falls off the tip!

When you hold your hand "motionless," the muscles in your arm are constantly making slight up-and-down adjustments. This ever-so-slight movement inches the hairpin along. The harder you try to steady your hand, the more corrections your muscles make, and the faster the hairpin walks!

Have a race with your friends. The one whose hairpin falls off first has the least steady hand . . . and loses the race!

Knife Suspension

Challenge: Support a glass in the center of four table knives, the handles of which rest on four glasses.

If you set up the knives before anyone can see them, people will be puzzled by the arrangement.

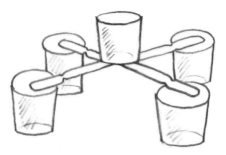

Arrange four glasses as shown. With the fifth glass in the center, support the knives as you overlap their tips. As you slip the fourth knife into position, raise the other three with your finger. The tips of all four knives end up slightly above the center glass which you can remove and place on top of the knives.

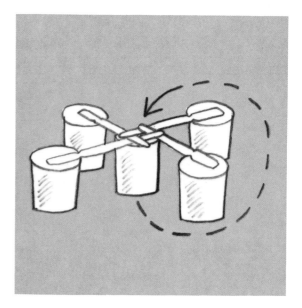

Fork Balancing-Act

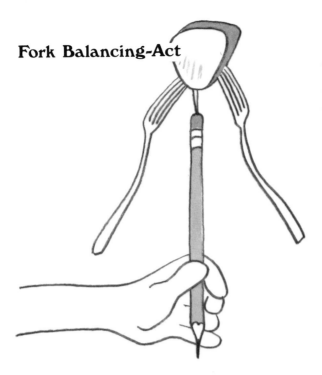

You can balance a thick piece of apple, pear, or potato on the point of a toothpick with the help of two forks.

Insert half a toothpick partway into the middle of the straight edge of the slice or wedge. Then stick two forks into the slice so that the handles hang down on each side as shown. Place the point of the toothpick on the eraser of a pencil. The fruit, forks, and toothpick should balance on the eraser!

If they don't, it's because the fork handles are too far from the pencil. Reinsert the forks with the handles closer to the pencil. If the slice tips so that one of the handles touches the pencil, move the other fork away from the pencil.

The fruit, forks, and toothpick make up a single unit that has a center of gravity—an imaginary point at which the pull of gravity seems to be concentrated. When you've adjusted the forks so that the center of gravity of the unit is directly below the point of the toothpick (the point of support), the unit is in balance. The whole setup will stay balanced even when you give it a gentle push to set it rocking back and forth or slowly rotating.

Sounding Fork

Piano tuners and scientists vibrate tuning forks with two prongs called tines to produce pure tones.

A dinner fork acts in much the same manner. Rap a fork on the table and quickly hold it close to your ear. The pitch of the sound you hear is determined by the mass of the tines.

Rap the fork again and touch the handle to the bone just behind your ear. The sound is much louder. The vibration of the tines is carried down the handle to the bone which conducts it to your inner ear. Some hearing aids work on this principle.

Rap the fork against the table again. This time firmly bite the handle with your teeth. The sound vibrations travel through your teeth and bones to your ear and now are really loud! No wonder the sound of the dentist's drill is so annoying!

Spoon Gong

If you rap a spoon against a table, the spoon vibrates. You hear some of the vibrations through the air as a clink. Other vibrations are too weak for you to hear . . . except with the help of a piece of string.

Tie the string to a spoon. Hold the end of the string tightly to the center of your ear, letting the spoon hang down.

Now rap the spoon with the handle of a knife. The weaker sound vibrations from the spoon travel up the string to your ear. You'll be surprised to hear the sound of a bell! Try the same experiment using an object other than a spoon. You may hear a chime or gong, depending on what's vibrating at the end of the string.

Spoon Flip

You don't think of a spoon as a lever, but you can use it as one. The bottom of the spoon's bowl is the fulcrum, the pivot point. The tip of the bowl is where you apply force. The end of the handle is where you do the work . . . to flip another spoon into a glass.

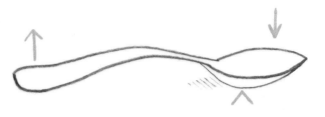

Set up the spoons and glass as shown and hit the tip of the bowl of the first spoon with your closed fist. If you've lined up the spoons and glass properly and hit the first spoon just right, the other spoon will flip over into the glass.

Salad-Bowl Solar Reflector

The inside surface of wooden salad bowls is often rounded without the flat section at the bottom usually found in plastic or glass bowls. You can use this curved surface as the base for a solar reflector.

Line the salad bowl with aluminum foil with the shiny side out, and glue the foil into place with rubber cement. (Rubber cement will not damage the salad bowl.) Position the bowl (perhaps with a modeling clay base) so that its inside surface is facing the sun. Place your hand opposite the center of the bowl and move it toward and away from the bowl until you can feel an area that's hotter than the rest. Be ready to jerk your hand away, because the sun's rays are being concentrated by the shape of the reflector and the temperature may be surprisingly high.

The efficiency of your solar reflector depends on the size and shape of the salad bowl and how smoothly you were able to apply the aluminum foil. The more nearly the bowl is shaped like the curved surface called a parabola, the more the parallel rays of sunlight will be focused on a small area.

Finger Boiling

Wouldn't you be amazed to see a glass of water boil with the heat from a hot finger?

It's a trick, of course, but the effect is so realistic, the water actually seems to be boiling!

Pour water into a glass until it is almost full. Then drape a handkerchief over it. Hold the handkerchief in place with a rubber band. Push down on the surface of the handkerchief over the water.

Now tell a friend to rub his finger on his clothing until the friction heats up the finger. Have him hold his finger under the glass. Hold the glass and the handkerchief with one hand while you push the glass downward with the other. Bubbles rise from the handkerchief and float to the top of the water as though the water were boiling.

Actually the bubbles are air forced up through the handkerchief. It looks so much like the water is boiling, your friend will be dumbfounded . . . until you give away the secret.

Quickly turn the glass upside down. The water stays in the glass because the tiny holes in the handkerchief are filled with water. (See Jar Puzzle, page 34.)

Glass-of-Water Puzzle

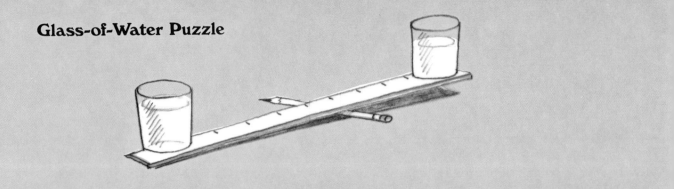

Place a 12-inch ruler on a pencil with six flat sides (its cross-section is a hexagon). Make sure that the 6-inch mark is directly over the pencil. Next, position a drinking glass at each end of the ruler and fill one of the glasses about three-quarters full of water. Slowly pour water into the second glass until the ruler tips to that side. You want the second glass of water to be just slightly heavier than the first glass.

Challenge a friend to predict what will happen when he puts his finger in the lighter glass. Will it remain lighter, or gain weight? After making his prediction, he puts his finger in the lighter glass. It becomes heavy enough to shift the ruler balance down on that side!

When he puts his finger into the water, he increases the volume by an amount equal to the volume of his finger under the water. It's as though he added that much extra water to the glass. No wonder it got heavier!

Sewing Supplies

Pin Piano

You can play delicate, charming music on
a piano made of pins!

Draw a line on a piece of wood and pound the first pin into one end of the line. Stick
another pin in the eraser end of a pencil and with it, pluck the pin in the board. It
vibrates, sending out a feeble sound. Don't worry, you'll make it louder later.

The pitch of the sound is determined by the mass of the pin above the board. At
regular intervals along the line, drive pins into the board. Tune them to the pitch of the
notes of the scale by adjusting the height of the pins above the board. You'll probably
have to cut off the pointed end of the pins for the higher notes with pliers because
you'll bend the pins when you hammer them into the wood.

Make the feeble sound produced by the pins louder by mounting the board on a box.
Cigar boxes were once used for this purpose, but they're scarce these days. Shoe boxes,
cardboard boxes, or any other box made of relatively thin material will work. Glue the
pin piano to the upside-down bottom of the box. The object is to transfer the vibrations
of the pins to the entire box and thus amplify the sounds.

A music box works on the same principle. Instead of pins, tiny reeds are vibrated by
pins in the proper position on a drum. As the drum turns, the pins pluck the reeds. The
entire music box is the amplifier.

82

Pin Touch-Tester

You'll be amazed at how the sense of touch varies over the skin of the human body.

To test the sense of touch, make a touch tester with two straight pins.

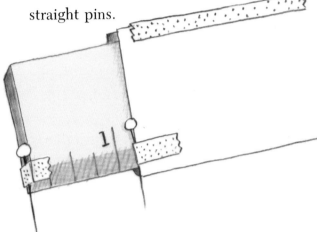

Fold a light piece of cardboard (an index card, for instance) in half. Tape a straight pin to one edge so that the pointed end of the pin protrudes about ½ inch beyond the folded edge. Insert a ruler into the folded card so that the point of the pin is at the edge of the ruler with the measuring marks. Tape the folded index card together so that the pin can slide along the ruler. Run the card to the end of the ruler and position another straight pin at the end of the ruler (or over the O mark if the measuring marks do not begin at the end of the ruler) so that it sticks out the same distance as the first pin. Tape the end pin in place.

Start with the two pins close together at the end of the ruler. Have someone close her eyes and touch the back of her hand with the tester. She will feel the touch of a single pin. Lift up the tester and move the sliding pin so that it's over the ¼-inch mark and touch her again.

Continue to move the pins farther apart and touch her each time until she can feel two pins. Make a note of the distance and the area tested. Now try another area, repeating the same procedure.

Areas of the body vary greatly in their sensitivity to touch. Test the front and back of the hands, arms, legs, back of the neck, forehead, tip of the nose, under the nose, middle of the back, and so on.

Spool Lunar Vehicle

A very long time ago someone figured out how to wind up a rubber band inside a spool and then make the rubber band unwind slowly to make the spool crawl across the floor.

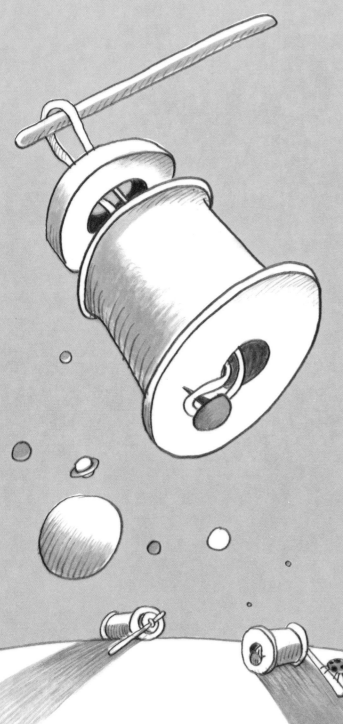

A modern version uses a spool of any size. Slip a rubber band, which is about the same length as the spool, through the opening, so that it passes from one end of the spool to the other. Anchor one end of the rubber band with a tack to the end of the spool. Slip the other end of the rubber band through the hole in a metal washer. The washer creates enough friction to keep the rubber band from unwinding quickly and yet is slippery enough to allow the wheel to turn slowly. That's why the washer is called a slipper. If you don't have a washer, you can make a slipper from the plastic of a refrigerator container or coffee-can top.

Into the end of the rubber band and through the slipper, put the last part—the drag. It can be a match stick, knitting needle, pencil, and so on. If the rubber band is not taut, wind it several times around the drag to take up the slack.

To energize your lunar vehicle, turn the drag to wind up the rubber band inside the spool. Set the spool down on the table. The drag keeps its end of the rubber band from turning. The twisting action of the rubber band is transferred via the anchor to the spool. With the right amount of friction from the slipper, the spool continues across the table until most of the energy you wound into the rubber band is released.

You can have races and battles if your friends also make spool lunar vehicles.

Spool Pulley

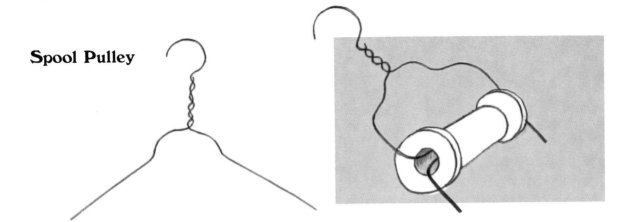

A spool is shaped like a cylinder with a flange at each end so that thread can easily be unwound from it as the cylinder turns.

This turning action makes a spool a convenient roller (called a sheave) for a homemade pulley.

Cut the bottom wire from a coat hanger and bend the two "legs" so that one goes through the hole in the spool and out the other end, and the other leg goes through the

hole in the other direction. Then bend the wires down on opposite sides of the spool to hold it firmly in place and yet allow it to turn freely.

With a screw eye, attach one spool pulley near your window and another to a friend's window next door. Run a loop of rope around both pulleys and tie the ends of the rope to a plastic basket. Be sure the rope is as taut as possible, to keep it on the pulley sheaves. You can now send messages and small items back and forth.

Produce

Apple Air Streams

Surprising things happen when you blow at a lighted birthday candle with half an apple in the way.

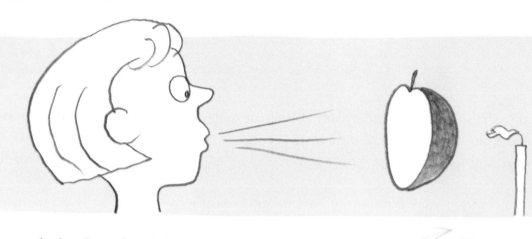

With the flat side of the apple toward you, the flame flutters toward the apple and is difficult to blow out. With the rounded side toward you, the flame moves away from the apple and is easily blown out. Why this difference?

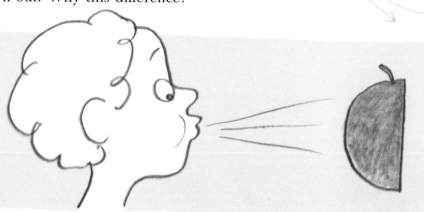

The flat side of the apple offers greater resistance to the air. The air swirls around it and actually flows away from the candle. The rounded side is more streamlined. The air streams flow around it more smoothly and come together, moving toward the candle. The combined air streams can carry the flame away from the wick more easily.

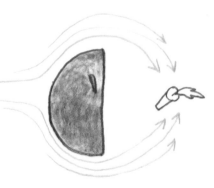

Cabbage Indicator

Hidden on the shelf of canned vegetables is a liquid that will tell you whether a chemical is an acid or its opposite, a base. The juice in a can of cooked red cabbage will do this by changing color!

Pour off the red juice into a pitcher as your supply of indicator. Put a couple of tablespoons of it into a small glass, add ⅛ teaspoon of baking soda, and stir. The color will change to green, showing the solution is a base. Add ½ teaspoon of vinegar and the solution will turn back to red, showing it is now acid.

Items in the supermarket are put into categories because they have something in common: fresh food, canned food, frozen food, and so on. In the same way chemicals are grouped together because of some of their common properties. Acids are one such group of chemicals. They can neutralize a base, and contain hydrogen. Bases are another group of chemicals that react with acids to form salts (still another group of chemicals), contain a chemical unit called a hydroxide ion, and often feel slippery or soapy.

Here's a chemical game for you to play. Below are common household chemicals that are either a base or an acid. Guess which is which and then test with your Cabbage Indicator to see how right your guesses were.

Ammonia, cream of tartar, vitamin C, aspirin, saliva, apple juice, borax, soda water.

Incidentally, among the other natural juices that change color when combined with acids and bases are those from carrot stems, beets, hollyhocks, rhubarbs, and cherries. As a science project you might try testing the colored juices from fruits or vegetables to see how they react to acids and bases.

Invisible Fruit Inks

Lemon, orange, grapefruit, and apple juices make pretty fair invisible inks. With a clean steel pen or fine brush, write a secret message with any of these juices as the ink. Usually the invisible message is written between the lines of another message that's not invisible.

When the ink is dry, it will be colorless on the paper. The recipient simply warms the paper with an iron or over a light bulb. The secret message will be readable!

Fruit juices (and other readily available liquids like milk, sugar water, and soft drinks) contain compounds of carbon that are virtually colorless when dissolved in water. On being heated, the carbon compounds break down, producing, among other things, carbon (the element)—which as you probably know is black. A similar chemical reaction takes place when you burn toast.

Banana Surprise

Imagine the amazement of a friend when you hand him a banana, which he peels only to find it has already been sliced into pieces! How can you slice the inside of a banana and not the outside?

Insert a threaded needle into one of the ridges on the peel and push it through under the skin to the next ridge. Pull the needle through, leaving a few inches of the tail end of the thread sticking out of the banana. Reinsert the needle into the same hole, and run it under the skin again to the next ridge. Pull the needle through again, leaving the thread in both the first and second holes. Continue around the banana like this until the needle comes out of the first hole you made. The thread now circles the banana under the skin. Gently pull the two ends of the thread, slicing the banana as neatly as with a knife. The more cuts like this you make, the more surprised your friend will be to find the banana sliced under the skin.

Celery Crunch

The crunch when you bite into a stalk of celery is partly due to the fact that its cells are full of water, which keeps the cell walls firm.

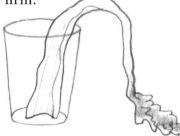

Place a stalk of fresh celery (with leaves on it, if possible) in an empty glass before you go to bed. The next morning the celery will be drooping and limp because the cells lost water by evaporation.

Now add some water to the glass. In a surprisingly short time the celery will straighten up again as its cells absorb water to replace what they lost.

To serve crisp celery, cooks keep it in water until just before serving.

Celery Tubes

To see how the water gets up a stalk of celery to the leaves, cut an inch or so off the bottom of a stalk of celery that has leaves at the other end. Put the cut end into a glass of water to which you have added food coloring or ink. In about an hour, the leaves and stalk will be streaked with color.

Cut off a small piece from the bottom and notice the colored spots along the edge. These are ends of the little tubes that conduct the water up the stem to the leaves. You can also cut the stem lengthwise and follow the tubes up into the leaves.

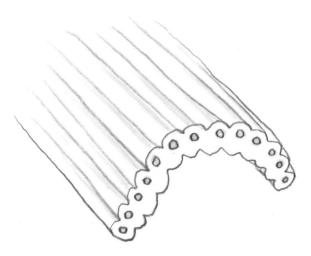

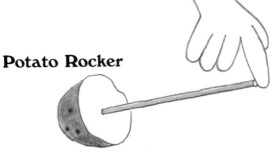

Potato Rocker

You don't ordinarily consider the weight of a potato when you eat it, but obviously it does have weight. When you combine that with its rounded shape, you have the base for a "roly-poly" toy.

Find a potato that's as close to a sphere as you can and cut it in half. Stick a plastic straw into the flat surface. When you hold the straw sideways to the table and let go, the weight of the potato base will right the straw, just like the roly-poly toys sold in toy shops.

For a young child, paste a cutout of a clown on the straw. When the toddler gets bored with the toy, you can cook it and eat it.

Answer to Problem Posed in the Introduction

Students were able to solve the problem of attaching a candle at eye level to a door (described in the introduction) because functional freedom allowed them to see that the candle could be placed in an empty box which became a shelf when thumbtacked to the door.

Potato Gun

With a slice of potato and a piece of rigid tubing, you can make a gun that works on the same principle as an air rifle but shoots pellets of potato!

The most important part of the gun is the tubing. It can be glass, plastic, brass, copper—anything that is straight and smooth. For a plunger find a piece of wood that is slightly smaller than the inside of the tubing.

Cut a ½-inch-thick slice from a large potato. Using the tubing in the same way you would a cookie cutter, cut out a potato plug with each end of the tubing.

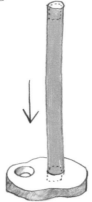

Slowly push the plunger into one end of the tubing to get the potato plug part way in and then push quickly. (Be sure you're not pointing the tubing at anyone.)

Because you've squeezed the air between the two plugs into a smaller space with the plunger, the air pressure inside the tubing forces the potato plug out the other end. The gun will make a popping sound and the potato bullet will land a considerable distance away.

Index

About the Author

Don Herbert is best known for his award-winning *Mr. Wizard* TV show of which he was the star for more than sixteen years. As Mr. Wizard, Don Herbert developed a reputation for entertaining young audiences with the magic and mystery of science in everyday living—a reputation he continues to build with his featured appearances on the monthly CBS after-school special *Razzmatazz*. In many states, the whole family can enjoy Mr. Herbert's talents on the local evening news, where he presents *How About*, a series of eighty-second reports on science and technology.

Don Herbert is the author and/or producer of ten books, forty-one classroom films, six science kits, and nine TV specials. He has been a guest many times on *The Tonight Show, Today, The Merv Griffin Show, The Mike Douglas Show, Dinah!*, and scores of local TV and radio shows. And remember the General Electric Progress Reporter? That, too, was Don Herbert.

Mr. Herbert lives in Canoga Park, California, with his wife, Norma.

About the Illustrator

Roy McKie is probably one of the best and most inventive cartoonists in America today. During the past twenty-odd years, he has done illustrations for nearly every magazine, advertising agency, and book publisher one could think of. But his biggest claims to fame are the children's books he has illustrated (and sometimes written) for Random House. One of his specialties has been illustrating joke and riddle books including *The Riddle Book, The Joke Book, The Sniff and Tell Riddle Book*, and several of Bennett Cerf's popular books of riddles.